Programming in C

John Gray

and

Brian Wendl

Department of Computing
Manchester Metropolitan University
UK

CHAPMAN & HALL
University and Professional Division
London · Glasgow · Weinheim · New York · Tokyo · Melbourne · Madras

Published by Chapman & Hall, 2–6 Boundary Row, London SE1 8HN, UK

Chapman & Hall, 2–6 Boundary Row, London SE1 8HN, UK

Blackie Academic & Professional, Wester Cleddens Road, Bishopbriggs, Glasgow G64 2NZ, UK

Chapman & Hall GmbH, Pappelallee 3, 69469 Weinheim, Germany

Chapman & Hall USA, One Penn Plaza, 41st Floor, New York NY 10119, USA

Chapman & Hall Japan, ITP-Japan, Kyowa Building, 3F, 2-2-1 Hirakawacho, Chiyoda-ku, Tokyo, Japan

Chapman & Hall Australia, Thomas Nelson Australia, 102 Dodds Street, South Melbourne, Victoria 3205, Australia

Chapman & Hall India, R. Seshadri, 32 Second Main Road, CIT East, Madras 600 035, India

First edition 1995

© 1995 John Gray and Brian Wendl

Typeset in 11/13pt Times by Columns Design & Production Services Ltd, Reading
Printed in England by Clays Ltd, St Ives plc

ISBN 0 412 55990 0

A catalogue record for this book is available from the British Library

♾ Printed on permanent acid-free text paper, manufactured in accordance with ANSI/NISO Z39.48-1992 and ANSI/NISO Z39.48-1984 (Permanence of Paper).

Contents

Preface

This book assumes that the reader has some previous experience of programming using a procedural language such as Pascal or a structured BASIC. It is suitable for use by students and also by commercial programmers who wish to increase their programming skills by learning to program in C. Readers meet full working programs starting in Chapter 1 and subsequent chapters introduce the various features of C in the context of other complete programs.

ANSI C is used throughout the example programs (ANSI stands for the American National Standards Institute).

Working on the premise that an understanding of the purpose of the constructs available within a language improve the learning of that language, each chapter begins with a problem and its solution, both as pseudo-code and as a C program. The solutions contain examples of the constructs and ideas which are to be introduced through the chapters. In the subsequent discussion of the solutions examples of the new constructs are emphasized and other interesting or novel features are brought to the reader's notice. Margin notes are also used to highlight important points and to give interested readers information on relevant points not covered in the text.

In several cases major examples are questions taken from the 'Programming in C' second-level degree course run at the Manchester Metropolitan University and here the worked solution and subsequent discussion are intended as indications of the style of answer expected. Needless to say, such solutions are by no means prescriptive; there are potentially many solutions to these problems. The Department of Computing at Manchester Metropolitan University has adopted the view that students should know the syntax of the language but this is of secondary importance. What matters is that they can apply their knowledge of the language in devising a solution to the problem.

This incorporation of examination questions is taken further by the inclusion of further such questions in the relevant exercises section within each chapter. Again, fully worked solutions to selections of these are given in the answers section at the back of the book.

The general organization of each chapter is as follows:

Introduction – a brief outline of the chapter contents
Problem – the context within the new constructs are introduced
Pseudocode solution – a semi-structured English statement of a solution
C program – a program based on the pseudo-code
Discussion – an investigation of the solution
Exercises – practical tasks involving problem solving and writing C programs

Language-specific features – introduces features which are specific to C
Summary – a concise review of the features covered in the chapter, acts as a revision aid
Further exercises – larger practical tasks involving problem solving and writing C programs.

A summary is given at the end of each chapter and this gives a generic, concise version of the constructs introduced during that chapter. This is included as both a reference and a revision guide; our view is that experienced programmers should expect that a language provides certain constructs and all they require is to determine the form of those constructs in C. For other readers we expect that, as they progress through the material and gain in expertise, they will need to review and remind themselves of earlier topics. Again the summary should facilitate this.

It was stated earlier that the book is primarily aimed at readers with experience of another block-structured language. One further feature of the book is that it does not over-burden readers with detailed C specific features unnecessarily. Each chapter has a separate section dealing with aspects, syntax or constructs which are specific to C. This separation should emphasize facets in C which are not commonly found in other languages.

Chapter 1

Introduction

OBJECTIVES

On completion of this chapter you will be able to:

- □ give a brief history of the C programming language;

- □ write a simple C program;

- □ use the fundamentals of the C language – keywords and base data types;

- □ use assignment and the arithmetic operators;

- □ deal with mixed type expressions;

- □ use constants;

- □ use simple input and output.

In this first chapter you will meet some of the fundamentals of the C programming language such as its set of keywords, creating identifiers and the declaration of base type variables. An example problem is used to illustrate the use of basic input/output, the base types and the application of some simple arithmetic operators. At various points in this chapter you will be prompted to type in either a program or complete sets of exercises. We suggest that you follow these suggestions as they are intended to help you to build up your competence in the use of an ANSI C compiler. Programming is a practical activity and it is through writing programs that you improve your abilities in this field.

ANSI – American National Standard for Information Systems – Programming Language C, X3.159–1989.

Writing a simple C program

This section is to introduce the ANSI C programming language. We present a brief historical context for the ANSI C programming language and then move swiftly on to discuss the parts of a simple working ANSI C program.

Note that throughout this book reference to the C language will be assumed to mean the ANSI C standard version.

A Brief History of C

What does C stand for? Well, actually nothing other than an indicator of where the language came from; yes, its predecessor was called B. The predecessor of B was called BCPL, and it is really here that we find the true origins of the C programming language.

BCPL was actually a subset of CPL developed at Cambridge and London Universities

In 1967, Martin Richards at Cambridge developed BCPL or Basic Combined Programming Language. This was a language used as a compiler writing tool and for other systems programming. BCPL had only one data type, the bit pattern and had many operations based on address arithmetic, useful for 'low-level' systems programmers.

In 1969 the UNIX operating system was being developed at Bell Laboratories, using assembler language. Ken Thompson designed the B language based on BCPL and used this at the Bell Laboratories to write the UNIX operating system for the DEC PDP-7 computer. Subsequently Dennis Ritchie incorporated some of the high-level aspects of ALGOL60, a strongly typed language, into the B language and hence along came C. Some 90% of the UNIX operating system for the PDP-11 computer was written using C and the portable UNIX operating system hit the world. With the explosion in numbers of personal computers and, more recently, powerful workstations running UNIX, C has increased in popularity.

The final strength came in the standardization of the C language through ANSI. This started in 1982 and was completed in late 1989, though compilers conforming to the various drafts of the ANSI standard were developed throughout this period. C thus shows the strengths of many good block-structured procedural languages whilst retaining its powerful set of operators and assembler like abilities.

Why not try to find out a little more about some of these variants. Look in the library of your local College or University.

There are also now several variants of C including C++, an object-oriented version, and, Concurrent C, a parallel processing version. C++ came about in 1984 by the addition of classes and is fast becoming an important commercial object-oriented language. C++ is also extensively used in the academic environment for both educational and research activities.

So, C is not a new language and its popularity arises from its use as the assembler language for the UNIX operating system. In this role low-level addressing, bit manipulation and assembler abilities have allowed it to become useful for system type programming on a variety of machines. These same facilities make it an ideal language for performing systems work on PCs.

C is a language that has a powerful set of operators. It allows expressions to be used wherever statements can be used and thus allows very terse, some would say, obscure lines of code to be written. It is very much up to the programmer to ensure that a compromise is reached between using these powerful features whilst producing readable code.

ANSI C programs written conforming to the standard should be portable. This means you should be able to compile the ANSI C programs on any machine that has an ANSI C compiler.

What do C programs look like?

Depending on your past experience of programming languages, C will look like Fortran at the outer level but more like Pascal at the inner level. C allows separate compilation where parts of a program can be kept in individual source files and compiled independently of each other. To build a run-time system, these compiled files are linked together via the linker, link-loader or whatever is used on your particular system. This has a speed advantage over the compilation of a single large file.

We will discuss this further when we look at C functions.

A C program is composed of 'external objects' – mainly **functions** and **global declarations**. External objects can be used throughout a program – there are also internal objects whose use is much more limited. Initially we will only use functions.

A function in C is the equivalent of Fortran's functions and subroutines and Pascal/Modula-2's functions and procedures. Function names are intended to encapsulate the purpose of the actions performed within them. The function `main()` is special – when your program is executed this is where execution starts and when this function ends the program is finished.

An example program:

Why not try to enter this program, compile, link and run. The way you achieve this will vary from machine to machine.

```
/* This is a simple program to illustrate some features */
/* of the C language. Note, C is case sensitive and */
/* so here everything is written in lower case letters. */

#include <stdio.h>

main()
{
        printf("Hello World\n");
        return(0);
}
```

Let us now examine the structure of the above program.

Comments

/*...*/

Comments are very important in documenting code. Notice how this is achieved in our examples.

Everything that follows the `/*` will be taken as a comment until `*/` is encountered which terminates the comment. The compiler will ignore everything between these comment markers. Be careful not to split these comment pairs or to attempt to nest them. You can use comments anywhere that white space, i.e. a space, newline and tab etc. would be allowed.

A preprocessor command

<code>#include <stdio.h></code>

The **preprocessor** is normally invoked as part of the call to the compiler
and it interprets any preprocessor commands before the actual compiler acts
on the source code. The # character in column one allows the preprocessor
to recognize preprocessor statements and the word immediately following
the # is taken to be the actual command. In this example the word `include`
is the command. The angle brackets ◇ inform the preprocessor to look in
the standard place (/usr/include on UNIX systems) for the given file. You
can probably guess that `stdio.h` refers to the standard portable input/output
library. The ending `.h` means header as these are known as header files. The
effect of this preprocessor command is to replace the command in the C
program with the contents of the file `stdio.h`, i.e. the original C program
becomes the concatenation of the file `stdio.h` and the function `main`.

Creating the function `main()`

<code>main()</code>

You will have met functions and procedures in other programming languages. All C programs contain the function `main()` somewhere in their
source code. This is a special function in that it tells the compiler the point
at which execution is to begin when the program is run. It follows from this
that there can only be one function called `main()` in any C program. In the
example above `main()` has no parameters; this is not always the case as you
will see when we discuss command line arguments for C programs. The
general form for functions in C is:

```
Return_Type Function_Name(parameter_list)
     {
             Statement1;
             Statement2;
             StatementN;
             return(Return_Value);
     }
```

Using a function

<code>printf("HelloWorld\n");</code>

`printf()` is a function prototype declared in `stdio.h` By including `stdio.h`
in this program we are able to use all the functions, and other objects, which
it contains; thus we are making use of a function to display some text on the
Visual Display Screen (VDU) or monitor. Notice that the call to use
`printf()` incorporates a parameter, namely the string of characters "**Hello
World\n**". The \n at the end of this string is a visible representation of a
non-printable character, in this case `newline`, i.e. \n in a string means move
the output cursor down one line and back to the start of that line. The \ is
used to mean escape or treat the following character in a special way and

there are a series of such 'escape sequences'. Where a string contains an escape sequence nothing of that sequence is actually printed, so if a string has \n then the literal \n is not printed, but the result is to move the cursor to the start of the next line of output. Every character in a string is significant and if you wish to print spaces around the words and other objects that you print you must make them part of the string.

The escape character can also be used to tell the compiler to ignore any carriage returns that are present within a string for example:

See Simple Input Output section later in this chapter for a more detailed review of these sequences .

```
#include <stdio.h>

main()
{
      printf("Hello World\");
      printf(" This is going to be a \
long string all on one line\n");
      return(0);
}
```

Returning a value from a function

```
return(0);
```

As a general rule, a function always returns a value and thus there is a need for a mechanism to achieve such a return. It should be clear that C provides this through the `return` statement. Now in our example program the only function in sight is `main()` and there is nothing to tell you what type of value it should return. Well, in C if there is no information on the type of some object then it is assumed to be an integer; thus we return 0. What happens to this value since there is no calling function? It is returned to the operating system, which may or may not use any such value (it depends on how you have invoked the execution of the program). To be consistent you should always have a `return` statement in any function except those in which you explicitly state that no value is to be returned (see Chapter 3 on Functions for further details).

Remember, we will discuss functions in greater detail in a later chapter.

Statement terminator

```
;
```

This is a vital part of C syntax, it is a statement **terminator** (cf. Pascal where the *;* is a statement separator) and must follow every statement in a C program. If you look at the example program you will see that the last statement is that of `return(0)` and it has a *;* after it. In C the *;* is not used in the same way as it is in Pascal or Modula-2 where any statement immediately preceding an END does not need a *;*.

Block Delimiters

```
{}
```

The { and } are to enclose the body of the function. They are also used to

C gives you greater flexibility within blocks, e.g. you can declare variables within any block.

group a number of simple statements to form a compound statement. Their purpose is similar to the BEGIN...END of Modula-2 and Pascal.

Exercises on simple C programs

1.1   How do you think you would print the character " as part of a string?

1.2   What do you think the following would output?

```
#include <stdio.h>

main()
{
        printf("Hello ");
        printf("World\n");
        return(0);
}
```

1.3   Write a C program which prints out the following message:

```
This is a very long line of output which also incorporates
the printable character " as part of its content.
```

Edit, save, compile, link and run your program.

Introduction to C fundamentals

Now that we have given you a brief history of C and shown you a very simple program it becomes necessary to introduce you to some of its underlying fundamentals, namely its character set, keywords and the creation of names or identifiers for use within programs. This information will help you to devise identifiers without clashing with the special set of keywords which C has and also make sure that you use characters which are known to C.

The C alphabet
The ANSI standard describes a minimum of 96 characters for the C language and these are:

```
a...zA...Z0...9!"#%&'()*+,-./:;<=>?[\]^_{|}~
```
space, horizontal tab, vertical tab, form feed and newline

Where the character set does not support 96 characters use **trigraphs** (see Appendix A).

They are all part of the ASCII character set, perhaps the most common set at present, and the 96 characters can be distinguished using seven bits. Although only the letters, digits and underscore are used in identifiers, all of the other characters are used both singly and in combination to form the rich set of operators that C provides. When considering what names to attach to identifiers you must avoid the use of the C special names or keywords.

Keywords in C

In common with many other programming languages C reserves to itself the use of a small number of words which it endows with special meaning and consequently programmers should not use them as identifiers. There are 32 keywords in C and they are:

auto	double	int	struct
break	else	long	switch
case	enum	register	typedef
char	extern	return	union
const	float	short	unsigned
continue	for	signed	void
default	goto	sizeof	volatile
do	if	static	while

Please note that all keywords are in **lower case** and **must** be written as such!

Many of these keywords should be familiar to you, in particular `for`, `while`, `do` and `if`. These should be recognizable as looping and selection control constructs and they should raise certain expectations about the kinds of things that C supports.

Creating identifiers

With the proviso that an identifier cannot be the same as a keyword the rules for creating identifiers are as follows:

- they must start with a letter (underscore is counted as a letter);
- this can be followed by zero or more letters, digits and underscores;
- the length of identifiers is theoretically unlimited but the standard states that only the first 31 characters will be used to distinguish identifiers.

For external(global) identifiers only the first six characters are used.

A simple problem

Having given you a little about what names to avoid and also told you how to create names for identifiers, the following problem will give you practice in using identifiers.

Converting values from Fahrenheit to Centigrade and vice versa

Write a C program which allows a user to input a temperature in either degrees Fahrenheit or degrees Centigrade. Your program should then convert that temperature into its appropriate value in the other scale and print out both the original value and its converted form. It is known that if the input is in degrees Centigrade the value will be a whole number whereas if it is in degrees Fahrenheit it will be a real number. Equally, when the temperature is converted, if the result is in degrees Centigrade then it should be a whole number and if the result is in degrees Fahrenheit it should be a real number.

A pseudocode solution

Looking at this problem, it should be apparent that there will be two inputs to the program, namely the value to be converted and its current scale. Let us assume the inputs to be a character to represent the current scale and the temperature. Thus a structured-English form of the solution could look something like this:

> Prompt user for temperature scale of input ['f', 'c']
> if temperature scale is centigrade
> > read a whole number into `CentigradeValue`
> > Fahrenheit = Centigrade * 9/5 + 32
> > write `CentigradeValue` " degrees C is " `FahrenheitValue` "
> > > degrees F"
>
> else
> > read a real number into `FahrenheitValue`
> > `CentigradeValue` = `FahrenheitValue` − 32 * 5 / 9
> > write `FahrenheitValue` " degrees F is " `CentigradeValue` "
> > > degrees C"
> end of program

This solution obviously assumes valid inputs and as such would not be very robust, however it will serve the immediate purpose, which is to identify the need in the solution to cope with values of differing type. Hopefully it is clear that there appears to be a need for three variables and that these variables would be used to hold different types of values, namely whole numbers, reals and characters. Thus a C program based on this solution and using these variables could be as follows:

```
/*************************************************************/
/* */
/* Program to Convert a whole number Centigrade value to */
/* a real number Fahrenheit value, or vice versa. */
/* */
/*************************************************************/

#include <stdio.h>

main()                      /* no command line parameters */
{
        int TemperatureScale;       /* to hold the character */
                                    /* entered for the scale */
        int CentigradeValue;        /* holds a positive or */
                                    /* negative whole number */
        float FahrenheitValue;      /* holds a positive or */
                                    /* negative real number */
```

```
                        /* start of the actual code */

        printf("\fEnter the Scale for the Temperature to be"
                " entered [f,c]...");
        TemperatureScale = getchar();
        if (TemperatureScale == C)
        {
                printf("\nEnter the value in degrees "
                        "Centigrade...> ");
                scanf("%d", &CentigradeValue);
                FahrenheitValue = CentigradeValue * 9 / 5 + 32;
                printf("\n\n%d degrees Centigrade is %f "
                        "degrees Fahrenheit\n\n",
                        CentigradeValue, FahrenheitValue);
        }
        else
        {
                printf("\nEnter the value in degrees "
                        "Fahrenheit...> ");
                scanf("%f", &FahrenheitValue);
                CentigradeValue = FahrenheitValue - 32 * 5 / 9;
                printf("\n\n%f degrees Fahrenheit is %d"
                        " degrees Centigrade\n\n",
                        FahrenheitValue, CentigradeValue);
        }
        return(0);              /* function which can be used to */
                               /* terminate C programs and pass */
                               /* a value back to the initiating */
                               /* routine or process. */

}
```

Let us now examine the structure of this program. The first point worth noting is that it contains some errors, not syntax errors but errors associated with things like the order in which the arithmetic in the expressions are done. The following discussion should help to correct these errors.

Characters are a subset of the integer data type

TemperatureScale = getchar();

In the original problem it was stated that the user would be asked to input the temperature scale of the value to be entered and that this would be a character. In the above program no character variables were declared, although there was an `int` variable called `TemperatureScale`. In fact this variable was used to hold the result of a call to a function called `getchar()`, which has a very character-based feel about it. So, is there or is there not a character type in C? Well, there is a type called `char`, which holds character

For any given implementation the data type `char` will be a subset of the data type `int` for that machine's character set, e.g. ASCII.

values and is used most frequently in string handling. The function `getchar()` actually returns a value of type `int`; hence the use of the `int` variable rather than a `char`. This function will be considered in more detail in a later section.

Assignment and comparison

                    `if (TemperatureScale == 'c')`

The `if` statement in the above program contained a condition controlling which of the alternatives to follow, i.e. `(TemperatureScale == 'c')`. There are four points here:

1. `==` is the 'is equal to' operator and **NOT** the assignment operator `=`. A very common source of errors in C is to use the assignment instead of the comparison operator. You will find that the assignment operator is valid in any expression where a comparison operator can be used and so there will be no complaint from the compiler.
2. An integer is compared with a character, and this is perfectly acceptable given the point made previously in the section on 'Characters are a subset of integers'.
3. `'c'` is a character whereas `"c"` is a string and though this may seem an obscure distinction later exposure to strings should convince you that it is important.
4. All conditions in C must be placed within parentheses (round brackets).

Arithmetic operators and precedence

                `Centigrade = Fahrenheit - 32 * 5 / 9;`

To correct the problem use parentheses as follows:

`(Fahrenheit - 32) * 5 / 9`

In the expressions used in the conversions, note that the arithmetic operators in use are `+ - / *` just as you would expect. There is also a further operator for whole numbers and that is the remainder operator `%`. This as you might expect gives you the remainder when one whole number divides another. The sample solution to the problem contains an error which relates to the order in which the various parts of a complex arithmetic expression are evaluated, namely:

```
Centigrade = Fahrenheit - 32 * 5 / 9;
```

You should have met tables of operator precedence before. C also has such a table and this can be found in Appendix B.

Here the evaluation will be done as `Fahrenheit - ((32 * 5) / 9)`, and thus `Fahrenheit - 17.0`. The result of this formula would be incorrect, e.g. for an input of 32.0 degrees Fahrenheit it would produce a result of 15 degrees Centigrade. In C, as with many other programming languages, the normal arithmetic precedence rules apply in that multiplication, remainder and division are done first and then addition and subtraction.

Mixed type expressions

C apparently uses the same operators for reals and whole numbers and it is left to the compiler to detect which form should be applied. Where the operands of an operator are of the same type, then it is quite clear that the compiler would choose to apply the operator for that type. In the conversion expressions above real and whole numbers are freely mixed and thus ought to raise the question which operator should be used? The answer is that within the expression the values are converted to be the same and so the appropriate operator is applied. The rules of this converted are a little involved but a rule of thumb is:

See Appendix C for a full discussion of conversion within expressions.

'convert the least accurate operand to the accuracy of the most'.

This effectively means integers become real numbers and, as you will see shortly, smaller sized variables become converted to the size of the largest in the expression. One point worth making is that conversion does not affect the value held in a variable, but within that expression a copy of that value is made and stored as though it was of the other type.

Casting or explicitly forcing variables to be of the appropriate type

```
CentigradeValue = (FahrenheitValue - 32) * 5 / 9;
```

If the various operands in an expression are converted into one type, what happens if the result of the expression differs from the type of some variable to which it will be assigned? For example, in the above program there is a statement of the form:

```
CentigradeValue = (FahrenheitValue - 32) * 5 / 9;
```

In the expression on the right hand side of the assignment the result will be converted into `float` type because of the involvement of the `float` variable `FahrenheitValue`. However `CentigradeValue` is an `int`, so what happens when we assign the `float` value to the `int`? Well, truncation occurs unless alternate action is taken. Truncation will merely ignore the decimal value of the `float` and assign the whole number part to the `int`. Unfortunately this is done implicitly by the compiler. If you wish to inform other programmers that it is your intention to transform the `float` value here into an `int` value then you should explicitly coerce the type by using the cast operator, e.g.

There is a fuller discussion of casting and coercion in Appendix C.

```
CentigradeValue = (int) ( (FahrenheitValue - 32 ) * 5 / 9);
```

Maximum values held by variables

There seems to be an implicit assumption in the program above that the values either typed in or calculated will be representable in the data types given. To bring this into focus the ANSI standard states that the minimum range for an integer will ±32k. If you entered a value for a centigrade temperature of 40 000 what would happen? The result is undefined, i.e. not predictable. Equally the standard indicates that the minimum range for a real number will be ±1 E37. In the case of an `int` if the values involved are

```
main()
{
long int BigInt;
double BigFloat;
long double
VeryBigFloat;
```

likely to exceed the values that can be represented by that data type then you can qualify the declaration of the appropriate `int` variables with the word `long`. This would provide you with an integer variable whose value is stored in a minimum of 32 bits. For `float` variables the problem is often less one of total value and more one of accuracy with regard to the decimal part of real numbers. Here C provides a type `double` to give extra precision and even further precision may be obtained by qualifying the `double` with `long`. The actual representations for `float`, `double` and `long double` are dependent on the actual implementation; they may even be allocated the same amounts of memory! However do not attempt to use `long float` as this is invalid.

What are the ranges for the various forms of numbers for the machine on which your compiler is running? There are two header files `<limits.h>` and `<float.h>` which can be found in the directory /usr/include on UNIX systems or in the 'include' directory of the C compiler on IBM PC and PC compatible computers. Why not discover the ranges for integers and real numbers on your machine by finding and reading the header files `<limits.h>` and `<float.h>`.

The use of constants in C

Good programming practice should suggest that there are several aspects of the program which use literal constants and that these should be extracted and dealt with as constants. The particular values involved here are the integer 32, the expression 5/9 and the expression 9/5. Remember from the earlier discussion in order to generate the correct values from the expressions they need to be real expressions, i.e. the operands should be 5.0 and 9.0. C provides two ways of creating constants, through the preprocessor and through the `const` qualifier.

The `const` qualifier is applied to a variable declaration which can be initialized at the point of declaration and cannot be changed through direct assignment thereafter. Unfortunately, such a qualified variable is not a true constant; its value can be changed through the use of pointers. Although it can be used to set up values for use as constants, you, the programmer, must apply a convention to ensure that those values are not changed. The way to create `const` qualified variables is as follows:

```
const int ConversionFactor = 32;
const float FahtoC = 5.0/9.0;
const float CtoFah = 9.0/5.0;
```

The preprocessor mechanism for creating constants is to create a simple macro using the `#define` command. The enormous volume of C code written before the ANSI standard came into force used this way of creating constants and this of itself is a compelling reason to understand this mechanism. Where a symbolic or true constant is needed in the code, e.g. the bounds of an array, then you must create such a constant through the pre-processor, e.g.

```
#define Conversion 32
#define FtoC 5.0 / 9.0
#define CtoF 9.0 / 5.0
```

The preprocessor is dealt with in greater detail in Appendix D.

Notice that there are no semi-colons after the value at the end of the line; this is because such commands are for the preprocessor and not the compiler. Given these simple directives the preprocessor searches through the code body for all instances of the string `Conversion` and replaces them with the value `32`, and deals similarly with instances of `FtoC` and `CtoF`. This replacement occurs before the code is sent to the compiler and so all identifiers used in `#define` directives will have been replaced by the relevant values.

Initializing variables

One general point to consider is that, given the variable declarations made in the above program, the value of all the variables at the commencement of the program will be unknown. This is the default form of variable declaration and is termed 'automatic'. It essentially indicates that the memory allocated to such variables need only be held while the variable is in scope and is released when that scope is ended. An alternative way of looking at this is to say that an 'automatic' variable gets memory when the block in which it is declared is executed and that memory is reclaimed when the block terminates. For simplicity consider a function as a block.

The term 'automatic' is often abbreviated to `auto`.

Simple input and output

```
printf("Enter the value in degrees Centigrade..> ");
scanf("%d", &CentigradeValue);
```

The function `scanf()` is used to read in the temperature value. `scanf()` should be considered as the complement to `printf()` for reading data into programs. Note that it uses a string to describe the format of the input and that it operates in reverse when compared to `printf()` in that it puts values into the variables which match the format specified in the string. In fact `scanf()` expects the addresses of the variables in which it is going to place values and that is why each variable in the example program is preceded by the `&` (this is the address operator). A common error is the omission of the `&` before the variable and this causes some strange problems in programs. Note that `%d` means an integer and `%f` means a real number and this is true for both `scanf()` and `printf()`.

There are a set of format specifiers which are used to indicate different data types in the `scanf()` and `printf()` functions:

```
printf ("A string
%s\n", Message);
printf("%d and
%c\n", Integer,
Char);
```

```
scanf("%f %f
%ld",&Real,
&Double,&BigInteger
);
```

**We suggest you look at
your manuals for
further details of the
format specifiers.**

%s	string		
%c	character		
%d	whole number	%ld	long int
%f	float		
%f	double	%lf	long double

There are other simple specifiers for the int s which allow you to display them as octal or hexadecimal values. As we are looking at the printf() statement it is as well that you should be made aware of the range of special character sequences which you can embed within its output string. You have previously met the \n which indicates that a carriage return and line feed should be printed. Here are some of the other useful sequences which you can use:

\a	ring the bell
\b	backspace
\f	formfeed
\n	newline
\0	null character
\\	backslash
\t	horizontal tab

Language-specific features

When discussing the topic of the base data types only the more common variants were introduced. For example a case was made for int, float, long int, double and long double. With respect to the int data type there are a number of possibilities that should be recognized. In particular these concern the use of signed, unsigned and short integer values.

Signed and unsigned integers

$-2^{15} = -32\ 768$
$2^{15}-1 = 32\ 767$
$2^{16} = 65\ 536.$

As might be expected these are concerned with whether the representation of an integer has a mathematical sign, i.e. whether a value can be solely positive or positive and negative. The advantage of an unsigned representation over a signed one lies in the range of positive values which can be represented. An unsigned integer represented in 16 bits can hold values in the range 0 to 65 536 whereas a signed integer could represent numbers in the range −32 768 to 32 677. So if you knew that a variable was only going to hold positive numbers and that the maximum would always be less than 65 536 you could declare it as:

unsigned int PositiveValues;
(or can be written just as unsigned PositiveValues;)

This is one of many aspects of C which are aimed at efficiency of execution, without this facility you would have to declare the variable as a `long int` which most likely would require more memory and hence more processing to retrieve and use within calculations. You can also declare `long int` variables as `unsigned`, e.g.

```
unsigned long int EnormousPositiveValue;
```
(can omit `int` part again).

Short integers.

In the same way that you can request C to use a bigger piece of memory to store an integer, you can also ask it to use a smaller piece of memory. Again the possible benefit from this would be a saving in memory which might be a critical limitation in some circumstances. One common use for `short int` would be a loop control variable where the maximum value of that variable was below 256. To declare a variable of this type write the following:

```
short int SmallValue;
```
(or just `short SmallValue;`)

You can of course create `unsigned short int` variables.

Now that your awareness of the number of possible forms of `int` declarations has been raised you should also know that the actual amount of memory that any variable gets is dependent on the implementation. The discussion above suggests that a `short` will get 8 bits, an `int` will get 16 bits and a `long int` will get 32 bits. However, different compilers allocate memory differently and it is possible for a `short` to get 16 bits and both `int` and `long int` to get 32 bits. C has a unary operator called `sizeof` which can be used to determine the number of bytes needed for a given type, e.g.

```
sizeof(char);
sizeof(double);
```

Check the memory sizes for the various data types that your compiler allocates. The ANSI standard guarantees that a `short` will be represented in a minimum of 16 bits, an `int` in mimimum 16 bits and a `long int` in mimimum 32 bits.

Summary for C base data types

The following shows a template for simple C programs.

```
#include <stdio.h>    /* preprocessor statements */

main()                /* no command line arguments */
{                     /* open block for function main */
```

```
                    variable declarations;

                    statement1;
                    statement2;
                    statementN;
                    return(integer);
}                              /* close block for function main */
```

- C has four data types:

    char – characters
    int – whole numbers
    float – real numbers
    double – double precision real numbers

- These specifiers can be applied to the following types:

    char — signed, unsigned
    int — short, long, signed, unsigned
    double — long

Volatile – the opposite to const, a hint to a compiler not to optimize certain instructions

- These qualifiers can be applied to the above types:

    const – identifier is initialized and should not be changed.

Operators and their precedence are discussed more fully in Appendix B.

- You have the following arithmetic operators:

    int   + – * / %
    float, double   + – * /

    The usual arithmetic precedence rules apply. You will meet other arithmetic operators as you progress through the book.

Conversion is dealt with in greater detail in Appendix C.

- The conversion rules for mixed type expressions are:

    broadly speaking the least accurate type is converted to the most accurate type, i.e.

    short < int < unsigned int < long int < unsigned long int < float
    < double < long double

- By default all variables are declared to have automatic storage, i.e. the memory for such variables is only held while they are in scope.

- scanf() and printf() are complementary:

– they use a string with embedded specifiers;
– the specifiers are associated with a list of variables following that string;
– `scanf()` requires the address of variables.

Exercises on the base data types

1.4 What are the ranges for the data types `int`, `float`, `double`, `short` and `long` on the compiler for your machine?

1.5 How many bytes does your compiler allocate for variables of type `int`, `float`, `double`, `shart`, `char` and `long`.

1.6 Write a C program to read in a character and a positive offset. Your program should then display the original character, the offset and the character transposed by the offset. (For those of a more intricate mind, make the character a letter and ensure that transposing the letter by the offset produces a letter of the same case, i.e. the letter after 'z' would be 'a').

1.7 Write a C program to experiment with type conversions such as assigning an `int` to a `float`, a `float` to an `int`, a `float` to a `double` and a `char` to a `real`. Print out the result of each operation and check the effect of the assignments. For example, what happens if you assign a `float` value greater than the maximum `int` value to an `int`?

1.8 Write a C program which prompts a user for a character and then displays the position of that letter in the ASCII character sequence (this is the character set supported by most machines). Your program must NOT use assignment in achieving this end.

Chapter 2

The control constructs in C

OBJECTIVES

On completion of this chapter you will be able to:

- □ use the selection constructs of if and switch to take decisions;
- □ use the conditional operator ?;
- □ use the looping constructs for, while and do...while;
- □ create and use conditional compilation;
- □ create and use complex expressions to assist in controlling decisions and loops;
- □ use the compound arithmetic operators.

In procedural programming languages the general view of the order in which the statements contained in a program are executed is governed by the concepts of sequence, selection and iteration. Sequence is the obvious notion that statement2 is executed when statement1 has been completed and that there is only a linear structure to the program. Incorporating the idea of selection allows a programmer to provide alternative paths within this linear structure and thus decisions, necessary to decide between the alternative paths, are included in the language. Many forms of processing require repeated application of the same operations on different data items and the concept of iteration meets this need.

The C programming language has several selection constructs, including if, switch and ? (the conditional operator) and a number of iteration constructs among which are for, while, and do...while. This chapter introduces these constructs through a variety of example problems and programs.

The selection constructs or how to take decisions

Consider the following problem:

A National Government collects income tax from all people in receipt of earned monies. The rate at which individuals are taxed is dependent upon

the actual amount they earn and a table is used to determine the actual tax to levy. The current version of that table is given below:

Income	Tax rate per pound	Base amount
0	0.00	0
3 000	0.10	330
5 000	0.12	530
10 000	0.15	1 130
20 000	0.25	2 630

Here a person is taxed in two parts and the calculation is made as follows. The base amount of tax is calculated by determining the band in which their gross salary falls. There is also an extra tax levied at a variable rate on the amount by which the salary exceeds the lower bound determined for the base amount calculation. For example a person earning a salary of £12 000 would be liable to £1130 base amount and £2000 * 0.15 extra tax.

You are asked to write a program which will prompt a user for their gross salary and will calculate and display the tax liability for that salary.

Structured-English solution
Prompt user for gross salary (whole number)
If salary in the range 0..2999
        TaxLiability = 0
Elsif salary in the range 3000..4999
        TaxLiability = 330 + ((salary - 3000) * 0.1)
Elsif salary in the range 5000..9999
        TaxLiability = 530 + ((salary - 5000) * 0.12)
Elsif salary in the range 10000..19999
        TaxLiability = 1130 + ((salary - 10000) * 0.15)
Else
        TaxLiability = 2630 + ((salary - 20000) * 0.25)
End-If
Display "The Tax Liability on a salary of " salary " is "
        TaxLiability

The program
```
#include <stdio.h>
#define DEBUG  /* used for conditional compilation */

main()
{
        const int BaseTax        = 0;
        const int BaseRate       = 0;
        const int BaseMinimum    = 0;
```

As tax rates are subject to frequent change it is a good idea to reduce the problems associated with modifying the program each time the rates change. Storing the rates as constants is one way to achieve this.

```c
const int BaseTax3to5        = 330;
const float Rate3to5         = 0.10;
const int Base3to5           = 3000;
const int BaseTax5to10       = 530;
const float Rate5to10        = 0.12;
const int Base5to10          = 5000;
const int BaseTax10to20      = 1130;
const float Rate10to20       = 0.15;
const int Base10to20         = 10000;
const int BaseTax20plus      = 2630;
const float Rate20plus       = 0.25;
const int Base20plus         = 20000;
int GrossSalary;                       /* holds salary read in */
int Balance;                           /* amount to be taxed   */
float TaxRate;                         /* rate at which to tax */
int BaseAmount;                        /* fixed amount of tax  */

                    /* start of main program */
```

Note the use of parentheses ( ) around the conditions or expressions for the if.

```c
printf("Please enter your gross salary ..> ");
scanf("%d", &GrossSalary);
if ((GrossSalary > 0) && (GrossSalary <3000))
{
        BaseAmount = BaseTax;
        TaxRate    = BaseRate;
        Balance    = GrossSalary - BaseMinimum;
}
else if ((GrossSalary >= 3000) && (GrossSalary < 5000))
{
        BaseAmount = BaseTax3to5;
        TaxRate    = Rate3to5;
        Balance    = GrossSalary - Base3to5;
}
else if ((GrossSalary >= 5000) && (GrossSalary <10000))
{
        BaseAmount = BaseTax5to10;
        TaxRate    = Rate5to10;
        Balance    = GrossSalary - Base5to10;
}
else if ((GrossSalary >= 10000) &&
            (GrossSalary < 20000))
{       BaseAmount = BaseTax10to20;
        TaxRate    = Rate10to20;
        Balance    = GrossSalary - Base10to20;
}
```

```
            else
            {
                    BaseAmount = BaseTax20plus;
                    TaxRate    = Rate20plus;
                    Balance    = GrossSalary - Base20plus;
            }
#ifdef DEBUG                    /* an aid for debugging */
            printf("\nBaseAmount %d TaxRate %f Balance %d\n",
                        BaseAmount,TaxRate, Balance);
#endif
            printf("\n\n\nWith a gross salary of %d ",GrossSalary);
            printf("your tax liability will be %8.2f\n\n",
                        ((BaseAmount == 0) ? 0.0
                         : (Balance * TaxRate + BaseAmount)));
            printf("\n\nHold screen..>");
            scanf("%d",GrossSalary);
            return(0);
}
```

Conditional
compilation.

Note the use of the
conditional operator ?
here.

Let us now examine the structure of the above program.

Conditional compilation

#define DEBUG

#ifdef DEBUG ....#endif

This is an extremely useful facility which should be recognized and incorporated into C programs as early as possible. Conditional compilation allows you, the programmer to specify which parts of program are to be incorporated in any build of an object file. The program above gives a simple illustration of a technique which can save hours when debugging code. When you create C programs embed `printf()` statements at appropriate points which will show you the value of variables at key points within a program, e.g. before/after function calls, after calculations etc. Surrounding these `printf()` statements with the conditional preprocessor directives `ifdef...endif` allows you to control whether the enclosed statements are incorporated into the object file created when the program is compiled. The method for controlling their incorporation or exclusion is to define a simple macro, DEBUG in the example above, and to omit it if debugging is not required.

While you are still debugging and testing the code include the print statements in the compilation; when you are happy with the code, don't edit the source code to either delete or comment out these print statements, merely delete the DEBUG definition so that the DEBUG macro no longer exists. This means that you can build your code and design in aids for checking and debugging rather than add them afterwards. Equally these aids can be left in the code without encumbering the run-time files; this can be a great help for subsequent maintenance!

Use of parentheses around expressions

The basic form of the `if` statement is:

```
if (expression)
        statement;
```

An integral value is one which is a whole number. This can be signed or unsigned, short or long, int or char.

The parentheses around the 'expression' are necessary. Expressions in C must return an integral value (remember that C has no concept of Boolean values, only zero and non-zero) and so the set of operators which are used for deriving such results must result in integer values. The logical operators are:

Operator	Purpose	Example
==	equality	`if (Divisor == 0)` don't divide
!=	inequality	`if (divisor != 0)` do division
<	less than	`if (Salary < MinSalary)` don't tax
<=	less than or equal	`if (Salary <= MinSalary)` don't tax
>	greater than	`if (Salary > MinSalary)` levy tax
>=	greater than or equal	`if (Salary >= MinSalary)` levy tax

Here's another reminder to be very careful about the equality operator, a common coding error in C is to use = when == was intended. The compiler will not detect this since wherever == can be used the = operator is always valid!

The Boolean operators

In the example program the expressions controlling the various `if` statements comprise two parts, i.e. a test for the GrossSalary being above one value and below another. The Boolean AND operator `&&` is used to link these two parts. Although extra parentheses have been used within the expression to make quite explicit each part of the expressions, they are not actually required. Good programming practice should indicate that this is another aid to the subsequent maintenance of the code. The full set of Boolean operators is:

Operator	Purpose	Example
&&	Logical AND	`(Age > 65) && (Sex = 'M')`
||	Logical OR	`(Input = 'a') || (Input = 'A')`
!	Logical NOT	`!((Input = 'y') || (Input = 'n'))`

Note how C uses the same characters in a variety of contexts, for example the & has been used as the address operator, and now && is the logical AND. Indeed you will see later that & can also be used as a bitwise operator. This places an onus on the programmer to be quite sure which operation is required and also that the operator chosen will apply the intended operation.

Experienced C programmers will use the logical NOT operator in ways which may be unfamiliar to readers of languages such as Pascal or Modula-2. Typically a programmer might expect an expression which checks that a variable has some value other than zero to be written:

```
if (value != 0)...
```

The C form of this would be:

```
if ( !value )...
```

This takes advantage of the fact that a value of zero from an expression is taken as false and negating that result achieves the same end as the more usual `value != 0`. You must remember that in C everything returns a value unless it explicitly indicates otherwise and this allows a programmer to omit steps which other languages require.

Various forms of the `if` statement.
The example program shows perhaps the most useful form of the `if` statement but obviously C supports the forms:

```
if (expression)          if (expression)
statements;                  statements1;
                             else
                             statements2;
```

Here `statements` can be one, two or many statements. Where there are two or more statements in the body of an `if` construct these must be enclosed within a pair of `{}`. A good rule for consistent programming style is to enclose the `statements` part of all `if` constructs within a pair of `{}` to make it quite clear that such a set of statements is associated with a specific `if`. The income tax program illustrates this style of programming. If this is not done then there is the possibility of the dangling `else` problem, as follows:

```
if (expression1 )
{
        if (expression2)
                statements1;
}
else
        statements2;
```

In this code fragment the indentation suggests that the `else` part is to be associated with the first `if`. However, the compiler will associate it with the second `if` because an `else` is always associated with the nearest previous `if` unless there is something to indicate otherwise. In order to achieve the desired association use the `{}` as follows:

```
if
    (expression1)
        if (expression2)
            statements1;
else
        statements2;
```

Note also that there is a `;` after the last statement in any block. This is mandatory and NOT optional as in Pascal or Modula-2.

The use of the conditional tertiary operator '`?` `:`'

```
((BaseAmount == 0) ? 0.0: (Balance * TaxRate + BaseAmount))
```

In the last `printf()` function call in the example program there is a somewhat strange piece of code which appears to produce a value of type `float` for the `%f` specifier. How is this achieved? It all revolves around the tertiary operator `?` which returns a value. Here is the general form for this operator:

```
(expression1 ? expression2 : expression3)
```

The first expression is evaluated and if that evaluates to non-zero then the second expression is executed; otherwise the third expression is performed. Here the expressions can be complex and have side effects other than the value returned. For example, you can include assignment as part of `expression2` or `expression3`, e.g.

```
((Char == 'Y' || Char == 'y') ? (Char = getc()) : (Char))
```

The code for the `printf()` statement in the income tax program can be represented as follows:

```
((BaseAmount == 0) ? 0.0 : (Balance * TaxRate + BaseAmount))
        exp1                exp2              exp3
```

Here `(BaseAmount == 0)` is evaluated and if it returns `0`, i.e. `BaseAmount` is not equal to 0, then the expression `(Balance * TaxRate + BaseAmount)` is executed; otherwise the value `0.0` is returned. The conditional operator `?` is only useful for choosing between two possibilities.

The `switch` control construct

This allows a programmer to choose one of a number of possible paths, where the choice is based on an expression which evaluates to an `int`. Once one path has been chosen the other paths are ignored. It provides a more elegant and readable way of listing options and their associated actions than a whole series of `if...else if...else if...` statements. However, as the expression must return an integral value, it may not always be possible to use the `switch` construct.

Here is a simple problem which makes use of the `switch` statement in the ensuing example program.

A program is required which prompts a user for a digit in the range '0...9' and even digits are transformed into the *n*th lowercase letter of the ASCII character set, odd digits are transformed into the *n*th uppercase letter and the digit 0 is ignored. Any non-digit input results in an error message. Thus entering the digit 2 would result in the letter B, entering the digit 9 would result in the letter i.

The program

```
#include <stdio.h>

main()
{
        char Value;          /* holds character read in */
        int Result;          /* indicator of end state  */
        int Transform;           /* holds transformed input */

                    /* start of main program */
        Result = 0;
        printf("\n\nEnter a Digit [0..9] ..> ");
        scanf("%c",&Value);      /* read in a character*/
        switch(Value)
        {
            case '0': {
                         Transform = '0';
                         break;
                      }
            case '1':
            case '3':
            case '5':
            case '7':
            case '9': {
                         Transform = Value - '1' + 'A';
                         break;
                      }
            case '2' :
            case '4' :
            case '6' :
            case '8' : {
                         Transform = Value - '1' + 'a';
```

The digit in `Value` is used to select which of the `case`s is activated.

There can be one or more `case`s associated with a set of actions

Note the arithmetic on `int`s and `char`s here.

\b is one of a series of
special characters for
use with the `printf`
statement. Several of
these are listed in
Chapter 1 or refer to
your compiler manual
for a full list.

```
                                                            break;
                                    }
                default   :  {
                                            printf("\n\nInput not a digit:");
                                            Transform = '\b';
                                            Result = -1;/* error ending  */
                                            break;
                                    }
                    }
                                                        /* int as char and int */
                    printf("Transform is %c  %d",Transform, Transform);
                    return(Result);
            }
```

Note that the `int`
Transform is printed as
both an `int` and a
char.

Now to examine some of the points arising out of this program.

The need for the `break` statement when using `switch`

break;

Without the use of the `break` statement `switch` becomes a multiple-entry
statement where the point of entry is determined by the `case` matched and
all the statements against all the `cases` after that point are executed. Placing
a `break` statement at the end of each set of actions associated with a `case`
ensures that only the code listed against a set of one or more `cases` is executed. The effect of `break` is to transfer the flow of control to the first statement immediately following the block of code which contains the block of
code containing the `break`, i.e. the first statement following the closing } for
the `switch` statement. It has to be said that you can use `break` within loops
but the same effect can be achieved much more readably and simply by
using structured programming techniques. There is a further discussion of
the `break` statement in the Language-specific section of this chapter.

The `default` case option

Though the aim of the `switch` is to give programmers the ability to list
clearly all the possibilities involved in evaluating the `expression`, there is
another option called `default` which is available to use as a catch-all. This
can be used as a route for trapping and dealing with errors, i.e. values
derived from the `expression` which do not match any of the explicitly listed
`case`s.

The expression switched must be an integer

Pascal and Modula-2
programmers should
note that ranges such
as 1..9 or 'a'..'z'
cannot be used as
case values.

The expression evaluated to produce a result for determining which `case` to
use must render an integral value. This places an obvious constraint on the
applicability of the `switch` statement. The values used for each `case` must be
both integral constants and unique. While the order in which the `cases` are
listed is not important, readability suggests that some logical ordering for

the `cases` would be sensible. The same reason can also be cited for making the last entry that of `default`. Note that you can have several `cases` listed against one set of statements.

Exercises on the selection constructs

2.1 Distinguish between those situations where you would choose to use the `if...else if` and the `switch` statements.

2.2 A simple program is required which advises users of the range of new cars which can be purchased for a given amount of cash. Here is one set of information, though you may wish to add your own. Where a buyer has less than £3000 then there are no new cars available, in the range £3000 to £4999 then a Lada or a Yugo could be purchased; in the range £5000 – £7499 then a Metro, a Maestro, a Fiesta or an Astra are available; in the range £7500 – £9999 an Escort, a Sierra, a Cavalier or a Rover are available. Above £10 000 then the program should advise a user to consult Classic Cars magazine. Your program should prompt a user to enter the amount of cash they have to spend and supply the appropriate information. Note that a user should be allowed to enter any whole number value.

2.3 Write a C program which displays a menu as follows:

    1 – Pride and Prejudice
    2 – Palgrave's Golden Treasury
    3 – ANSI C Standard
    4 – English Oxford Dictionary.

    Choose a book [1...4] ...

Your program should read in the number of the book chosen. If the choice is book 1 your program should print 'You are lover of English literature', if book 2 then print 'You like poetry', if book 3 then print 'You like manuals', if book 4 then print 'You are a seeker of knowledge'. If any other input is given then an appropriate error message should be given.

The iteration or looping constructs

As with many procedural languages C incorporates looping constructs for situations where the actual number of iterations required is known or can be determined, this is the `for` looping construct, and also where the actual number of iterations is unknown or indeterminate. In this latter category there is a `while` construct for instances where there may be zero, one or more iterations and a `do...while` construct for cases where at least one or more iterations may be required. It is of course possible to use the `while` or the `do...while` in situations where the actual number of iterations is known and to use the `for`, with adequate restraint, in situations where the number of iterations is unknown but the efficiency and sensibility of such actions may well be questionable.

Read the following problem and then examine the ensuing example program. This is a contrived example which incorporates all three of the looping constructs in one program. The purpose is to illustrate the syntax of these constructs.

The problem

You are asked to write a C program which sums a set of whole numbers entered by a user and calculates their average. The program should prompt the user for the number of values which are going to be entered. For the good of your soul you are asked to provide a solution which provides the choice of using any of the three looping constructs. Special care should be taken to cope with the situation where the number of values entered is 0.

The program

```
#include <stdio.h>

#define WHILE 0
#define REPEAT 0
#define FOR 1

main()
{
        int Number;
        int Count;
        int Sum = 0;
        int Value;

                        /* start of main program */

        printf("\n\nHow many numbers to process ..> ");
        scanf("%d", &Number);
        if (Number == 0)
        {
                printf("\n\nNo numbers to be entered : "
                        "program ends here.\n\n");
                return(-1);
        }
#if FOR
        for ( Count = 1; Count <= Number; Count++)
        {
```

Use conditional compilation to determine which of the looping constructs is to be incorporated into the executable file for any one run.

Executing the `return` *statement here effectively terminates the program*

```
            printf("\nEnter number %d ..> ",Count);
            scanf("%d", &Value);
            Sum += Value;
        }
#endif
#if WHILE
        Count = 1;
        while (Count <= Number)
        {
            printf("\nEnter number %d ..> ",Count++);
            scanf("%d", &Value);
            Sum += Value;
        }
#endif
#if REPEAT
        Count = 0;
        do
        {
            printf("\nEnter number %d ..> ",++Count);
            scanf("%d",&Value);
            Sum += Value;
        }
        while (Count < Number);
#endif
        printf("\n\nThe Sum of the %d values read in = %d ",
                    Number,Sum);
        printf("and their average was %8.2f\n\n",
          ((Number == 0) ? 0.0 :(float)Sum / Number));
        return(0);
}
```

+= here is an example of a compound assignment operator

`Count++` means add 1 to `Count` after it has been used in the `printf` statement.

`++Count` means add 1 to `Count` and then use it in the `printf()` statement.

Note the use of the conditional operator ? to protect against division by 0.

Coerce the `int` Sum to be a `float` so that real number division occurs

Now to discuss some aspects of the program.

While/do ...while very like WHILE and REPEAT...UNTIL

These two looping constructs are very similar to their counterparts in Pascal/Modula-2 although you should note that the do...while and the REPEAT...UNTIL have opposite terminating logic, i.e. for the do..while you continue executing the statements in the loop while the terminating condition is true whereas in the REPEAT...UNTIL you continue to execute the statements in the loop until the terminating condition becomes true. Note that in their use in the example program the loop control variable is modified when it is being used within some other statement, in this case the printf(). This is characteristic of the use of the pre/post-increment/decrement operators in C. After all, why include redundant statements? The point to be quite clear about in these examples is that in the while loop

Count is incremented after it is used in the print statement whereas in the do loop Count is incremented before it is used in the printf().

Compound assignment operators

```
Sum += Value;
```

Another type of operator introduced through this example program is the compound assignment operator, here C again allows the programmer to write more concise code. Compound operators allow a programmer to assume the use of the variable on the left hand side of an assignment statement as part of the expression on the right hand side (RHS). The simplest example is the common increment statement:

```
Count := Count + 1;
```
can be expressed as Count += 1;

Here the += assumes that Count is the first operand on the RHS of the assignment. There are a set of such compound operators and these are as follows:

Compound assignment operator	Purpose
Count += Value;	Count = Count + Value;
Count -= Value;	Count = Count - Value;
Count *= Value;	Count = Count * Value;
Count /= Value;	Count = Count / Value;
Count %= Value;	Count = Count % Value;

The increment/decrement operators

```
printf("\nEnter number %d ..> ",Count++);
```

C has a pair of operators ++ and – which can be applied to a single operand and their effect is to increase or decrease the value of that operand by one unit. Here we will look at their application to numeric values and in Chapter 4 we will examine their effect on other values.

In the example piece of code there is an int variable called Count which is the operand for the increment operator ++. The explanation of the printf() statement is that the text Enter number is placed in the print buffer, the current value of Count is used to replace the %d format specifier, the value of Count is increased by one, the text ..> is added to the print buffer and the buffer contents are displayed on the screen. Notice that the current value of Count is used before it is incremented. This is because the ++ operator is placed after its operand, i.e. post-increment. Both operators have a pre- and a post-increment/decrement form, e.g.

```
      Count = 10;
(a)   printf("\nCount = %d",Count++); /* output is 'Count = 10' */
(b)   printf("\nCount = %d",++Count); /* output is 'Count = 12' */
(c)   printf("\nCount = %d",--Count); /* output is 'Count = 11' */
```

```
(d)   printf("\nCount = %d",Count--); /* output is 'Count = 11' */
```

Example (a) illustrates the post increment form of the ++ operator and here the current value of the variable Count is used in the printf() statement, i.e. 10. At the end of that statement the value of Count is 11.

Example (b) shows the use of the pre-increment operator and here the current value of Count is incremented by one BEFORE it is used in the printf() statement; thus it was 11 at the end of the previous statement and now we add one to it before using it in the printf so that its value is 12 when printed.

Example (c) illustrates the pre-decrement operator – and here the value of the variable Count is decremented by one BEFORE the variable is used in the printf() statement; hence it appears as 11 in the output.

Example (d) shows the use of the post-decrement operator and here we decrement the variable after using it in the printf() statement thus it appears as value 11 in the output but its actual value at the end of the statement is 10.

It is important to understand the sequence in which the pre- and post-increment/decrement operators are applied in these simple expressions because choosing the incorrect form of operator will have exactly the wrong effect in your code.

The semicolon and the do...while

There is a small but syntactically important point to make with regard to the do...while construct: the semicolon after **do....while (Expression);** is necessary, not optional! Again looking at other block-structured languages the need for a ; after the appropriate UNTIL clause depends on the context. These syntactic differences concerning the ; between C and other languages are centred around the purpose of this bit of syntactic sugar. In effect C uses the ; as a statement terminator and a programmer must use this to tell the compiler where a statement ends, whereas other languages use it as one of several statement separators, only one of which is needed to indicate the break between two statements.

Refer to the example program for a comparison of the same loop expressed using the for , while and do...while constructs.

The for construct

This is sufficiently different to warrant some expansion. The general form of this construct is:

```
for (initialization part; testing part; modification part)
          statements;
```

Any of the three components of the for loop can be omitted if there is no action for that component.

This one expression encapsulates all the usual looping requirements, but it separates them into three distinct parts. Thus you can initialize the loop control variable, describe the test for loop termination and state the size of the step for each iteration. However, you can go much further than this because in each part you can specify more than is needed to control the loop. Examine this example code fragment:

```
for (count = 1, sum = 0; count < size;
              average = (float) sum / (float) count, count++)
{
      scanf ("%d", &value);
      sum += value;
}
```

This simple code fragment calculates both the sum and average of a series of integers. Note that sum is set to zero in the initialization part of the for loop and that the average at each point through the loop is calculated in the modification part of the loop. This is of course a little unrealistic, but you will see much more beneficial uses of this facility when you meet arrays of characters and numbers.

The use of the increment/decrement operators for the loop control variables is commonplace. It should be obvious to you that the richness of the operator set allows C code to become terse and truncated. Learn to read code of this nature because it is usual style for practising programmers.

Language-specific features

The comma operator

In the code fragment illustrating multiple initialization and updating within the for construct the three parts of the for expression are separated by semicolons. Within each part where there are several statements each such statement is separated by a comma and here the comma is an operator. Effectively the comma operator allows the programmer to lump together a series of expressions separated by commas and the value returned by the series of expressions is the value returned by the last one in the series. This may seem somewhat obscure but it has its uses.

Jumps within blocks of code

Using the break statement within the switch is one form of this ability to jump out of blocks of code. break can also be used within loops and the if statement to ensure that execution of those statements terminates.

```
for (Count = 0, CharCount = 0; Count < = 9; Count++)
{
      scanf ("%c", &Char);
      if (Char == 'Q')        /* Q for quit now */
      {
            break;
```

```
        }
        else
        {
                CharCount++;
        }
}
```

Here is a companion statement, `continue`, which allows a programmer to stop processing a specific iteration of a loop and begin the next one, e.g.

```
for ( count = 0; count < 10; count++)
{
        if !(sum)     /* sum = 0 so skip this iteration  */
        {
                continue;
        }
        sum   += count;
}
```

The other statement available for jumping around code is the `goto` and associated labels. Good programming practice eschews the use of this construct and with the range of other facilities in C for jumping out of loops etc., one could question its inclusion.

Infinite loops in C
There are a number of application areas where it is necessary to start an infinite loop. Such can easily be achieved with any of the looping constructs, e.g.

```
for (;;)            while (1)      do
                                   while(1);
```

Notice that the `for` loop example shows that no action is required for any of the controls and so they are all omitted. This results in a condition which contains only ; i.e. `(;;)`. You must include the relevant ; when you omit a component of the `for` loop.

Summary for control constructs

• The selection constructs are as follows:
```
        if (expression)                 if (expression)
                statements;                 statements1;
                                else
                                    statements2;
```

```
if (expression1)
        statements1;
else if (expression2)
        statements2
else if (expressionN)
        statementsN;
else
        statements;


switch (expression)
{
        case const1 : {statements1; break; }
        case const2 : {statements2; break; }
        case constN : {statementsN; break; }
        default :{ statements; break; }

}
```

- The conditional operator:

```
(expression1 ? expression2 : expression3)
```

- The looping constructs are:

```
while (expression)              do
{                               {
        statements;                     statements;
}                               }
                                while (expression); |


for (initialization part ; test part; modify part)
{
        statements;
}
```

The pre- and post-increment/decrement operators can be applied to integral values and are summarized as:

++a	use incremented value of variable a
a++	use value of variable a then increment
--a	use decremented value of variable a
a--	use value of variable a then decrement

Exercises for the looping constructs

2.4   British Rail has a somewhat complex pricing arrangement in that it has a set of standard fares which vary between Friday and other days. The most expensive tickets are those purchased for travelling on a

Friday and a ticket for travelling on any other day costs 20% less than the Friday fare for the same journey. British Rail also allows a variety of discretionary reductions for students (25%) and senior citizens (33%). Given that the standard Friday fare from Manchester to Carlisle is £26.00, write a C program which extracts the requisite information from a user and tells them what the cost of a ticket to Carlisle would be. (Consider the use of complex expressions here!)

2.5 Write a C program which reads a series of characters from the keyboard and calculates the number of upper case letters, lower case letters, digits, space, control characters and punctuation characters in the series. Your program should prompt the user for the number of characters which are going to be presented and, at the end of the character input, should display the number of each type of character and its percentage of the total number of characters entered.

2.6 Why does C incorporate the pre- and post-increment/decrement operators? Investigate their actions by writing a C program which incorporates the following code:

```
for (count = 0; count <= 10; printf("count = %d\n",++count))
              ;
for (count = 0; count <= 10; (printf("count1 = %d\n",count++))
              ;
```

Is there a difference between the output of the two code fragments?

Chapter 3

Functions in C

OBJECTIVES

On completion of this chapter you will be able to:

- ☐ use functions, parameters and function prototypes;

- ☐ use functions from separate files to implement modular design and programming;

- ☐ create and use header files;

- ☐ explain variable scope and the storage classes, automatic, static and extern.

In the previous chapters you have already met some functions (e.g. printf() – used to print to the screen) which were included with the header file <stdio.h>. This chapter is concerned with creating and using your own functions and function libraries. We will begin with an outline of the basic function structure and then go on to apply this as the unit of reusable code to implement the top-down solution of a problem. We will then extend your knowledge of the types of storage used both within functions (local) and globally (external). We will look at issues affecting the scope of variables and how this can be used to implement problem solutions.

   Along the way we will explore how the use of functions can enable programming team members to work independently on the same project by examining those features of the C language which support reusability and encapsulation, also found in languages such as Modula-2. This leads us on to explore other C storage classes and to review how scoping and parameter passing can be used to produce modular code.

Functions and parameter passing

This section introduces functions and parameters with a particular emphasis on their use in implementing top-down solutions to problems. In C the function is used in a similar way to Fortran's subroutines and functions and Pascal/Modula-2's procedures and functions.

The basic structure of a function is as follows:

```
return_type  function_name (parameter declarations, if used)
{
        declarations;

        statements;
}
```

The problem

With this basic structure in mind let us now take a look at a problem which is solved in a top-down manner allowing parts of the solution to be mapped onto function calls:

A program is to be written which presents the user with a simple menu offering the basic functionality of a simple calculator. The user can select to add, subtract, multiply or divide two input numbers. The result is displayed. In addition the user can select to add or subtract the result of the last calculation to/from memory. The program continues until quit is selected.

Structured-English solution

Do

        Display Menu
        Get user option
        calculate or store result

             If option == 'A' then do addition
             Elsif option == 'S' then do subtraction
             Elsif option == 'M' then do multiplication
             Elsif option == 'D' then do division
             Elsif option == '+' then add to memory
             Elsif option == '−' then subtract from memory
             Elsif option == 'R' then show memory
             Elsif option == C then clear memory
             Elsif option == 'Q' then indicate termination
             Else prompt incorrect option
                End

While not quit chosen

The program

```
#include <stdio.h>

main()
{
            /* Give function prototypes */
        char process_nums(void);
```

```
        void display_menu(void);

        char Option;

        printf("\nWelcome to the calculator program\n");
        do
        {
                display_menu();
                Option = process_nums();
        } while (Option != 'Q');


}


void display_menu(void)
{
        printf("\nPlease enter one of the following options...\n");
        printf("\nA - to add two numbers\n");
        printf("S   to subtract two numbers\n");
        printf("M   to multiply two numbers\n");
        printf("D   to divide two numbers\n");
        printf("+   to add last result to memory\n");
        printf("-   to subtract last result from memory\n");
        printf("R   to recall memory\n");
        printf("C   to clear memory\n");
        printf("Q   to quit\n");
        printf("\n>>>>> ");
}


char process_nums(void)

{

                /* function prototype */
        double do_sum(char);

        char Option;
        static double result, memory;

                while( (Option = getchar()) == '\n');
                switch(Option)
                {
                        case 'A':
                        case 'S':
                        case 'M':
                        case 'D': {
```

```
                                result = do_sum(Option);
                                break;
                                }
                        case '+': {
                                memory += result;
                                printf("\n>>>Added to memory\n");
                                break;
                                }
                        case '-': {
                                memory -= result;
                                printf("\n>>>Subtracted from memory\n");
                                break;
                                }
                        case 'R': {
                                printf("\n>>>Memory holds.. %0.2lf\n",
                                memory);
                                break;
                                }
                        case C: {
                                memory = 0;
                                printf("\nMemory cleared\n");
                                break;
                                }
                        case 'Q': {
                                printf("\n Leaving calculator, bye\n");
                                break;
                                }
                        default: printf("\n>>>Invalid option, try
                                                        again\n");

                }
        return(Option);
}


double do_sum(char option)
{
                /* Function prototype */
        double get_number(void);
        double result = 0;
        double Number_1 = 0, Number_2 = 0;

        switch(option){
                        case 'A': {
                                Number_1 = get_number();
                                Number_2 = get_number();
                                result = Number_1 + Number_2;
```

Note that this could have been written more tersely as
```
printf("\n>>>Answer
is.. %0.2lf\n",
result =
get_number() +
get_number());
```

```
                                    printf("\n>>>Answer is.. %0.2lf\n",
                                    result);
                                    break;
                                    }
                    case 'S': {
                            Number_1 = get_number();
                            Number_2 = get_number();
                            result = Number_1 - Number_1;
                            printf("\n>>>Answer is.. %0.2lf\n",
                            result);
                            break;
                            }

                    case 'M': {
                            Number_1 = get_number();
                            Number_2 = get_number();
                            result = Number_1 * Number_2;
                            printf("\n>>>Answer is.. %0.2lf\n",
                                    result);
                            break;
                            }
                    case 'D': {
                            Number_1 = get_number();
                            Number_2 = get_number();
                            result = Number_1 / Number_2;
                            printf("\n>>>Answer is.. %0.2lf\n",
                                    result);
                            break;
                            }
                    }
            return(result);
}

double get_number(void)
{
        double number = 0;

        printf("\nInput a number>>> ");
        scanf("%lf",&number);
        return(number);
}
```

Let us now examine the structure of the above program.

Function prototypes

```
char process_nums(void);
void display_menu(void);
```

This is a feature of the language which is new to the ANSI standard. Notice that the functions to be used in `main()` have not yet been defined (in the case of functions you can treat defined as meaning implemented) and so the compiler cannot check whether the functions are being called with the correct parameter types and whether the function's return value (if any) is compatible within an assignment or an expression. So then, the first prototype says that `process_nums()` accepts no parameters and returns a value of type `char`. It is important that the void type be included if no parameters are expected as otherwise the compiler will assume that the program is non-ANSI and not perform any function call checking. The reason for this is that the ANSI compilers are designed to be compatible with the previous K+R versions of C. The reason is simple, there is much C code already written out there and programmers are not going to be prepared to convert it all to ANSI.

The second prototype shows that the function `display_menu()` not only accepts no parameters but also that it has no return value. This makes the function more akin to a Fortran subroutine or a Pascal/Modula-2 procedure.

Note also that the function prototypes are part of `main()` which implies that these routines will be used only within `main()`. Had the function prototypes been declared before `main()`, i.e. external to `main()`, then all functions in that file could have used the functions without further declaration and the compiler would have checked the type compatibilities for each subsequent invocation. It is recommended that you declare the function prototype within each function which will call it, even though it is common practice to declare all function prototypes at the start of the file (externally).

K+R stands for Kernighan and Ritchie who wrote the definitive book *The C Programming Language* which defined the C language pre ANSI.

Function parameters

```
double do_sum(char);
```

Here we have declared another function prototype but this time within the function `process_nums()` which is to use it. There are two reasons for doing this. First, the prototype is needed because the function is defined later in the file and thus, when the function `process_nums()` is compiled, the compiler will not yet know of this function and will therefore be unable to enforce type checking for the parameters and return type. Second, `process_nums()` is the only function to call `do_sum()` and so the prototype can be placed within the function rather than externally.

Let us step back a little and consider how parameter passing is achieved in the C language.

All parameters in C are passed by value, that is, the parameter is treated as a local variable within the function which holds a copy of the actual parameter passed in. This would imply that a function cannot change the value of the actual parameter passed into the function from the part of the program calling it. There is a mechanism in which a call by reference can be achieved akin to a VARiable parameter in Pascal/Modula-2. However, we will consider this mechanism in a later chapter. So, when do_sum() is called from process_nums():

result = do_sum(Option);

a copy of Option is taken and used within do_sum().

Function variables

```
char process_nums(void)
{
char Option;
static double result, memory;
```

Remember, parameters passed into functions are copies passed from the calling environment and are treated as local variables. So what about local variables defined within the function body? You can see in the above code fragment that Option is a local character variable. It has the storage class 'automatic' and will exist only for the duration of the function call. This is the usual storage class you will encounter but beware, you must not assume that a local variable has an initialized value; in fact it will most likely contain garbage. It is good programming practice to initialize variables explicitly.

Remember you met the 'automatic' storage class in Chapter 1.

The second variable definition is different and is best explained by taking a look at how the variables result and memory were used in the function process_nums(). The result variable was used to accept the returned value from do_sums() as **result = do_sums(Option);**

We have implemented a memory capability for the calculator which means that we must always know, i.e. store, what the result of the last calculation was. This could not be held in an automatic variable as the value would be lost on leaving the function. However, if a variable is of storage class **static,** then the storage exists between function calls and the same value is held until next accessed from within this function. Similarly the static variable memory is required to exist between function calls as otherwise the memory value would be lost. You can see that this mechanism provides a simple solution to the need for local variables which don't lose their value between successive invocations of a function.

Another approach would have been to pass the result and memory variables into the function as a call by reference and so update the value within the routine. The problem with this is that these variables could then have been altered in the calling environment, even if accidentally, and this is undesirable. Good programming technique demands that variables are kept as local as possible to avoid any side effects and to make efficient use of storage.

Yet another approach, all too often used, would have been to define these variables outside of any functions, i.e. globally. This would mean that any function defined in the same file after this definition would see the variable. Clearly, this is bad practice, as there is then no control over use of the variable. This may not be apparent to you now, but if you are working in a team, global variable control becomes very critical, as you do not know who in the team has written a function to access such global variables. In reality, global variables are sometimes used, but only when a number of functions expect to use a large number of identical variables. In such a case the number of parameters for a function may become very large and unmanageable. Global variable access is slightly more efficient than local variable access, but should only be used if you cannot find another way around.

One further thing to note about static function variables is that they are always initialized to zero, unlike automatic local variables which have no initialized value.

Return values

In C the function is assumed to return the type `int` unless explicitly redefined. We have used the return type `void` to mimic subroutines and procedures of other programming languages, but a few words of advice are worth giving here. It is good practice always to have a return value which can either be the required return value, e.g. if expecting a character returned, or indicate success/failure. It is usual to write C functions which return zero if successful and −1, or some error code, otherwise.

Alternatively, the return value can be from any expression, so for example **return(A > B)** will return 1 if true and 0 if false.

Look up some of the library functions in your C manual to see what return values they give and what their significance is.

Function names

Notice that in the program all functions are defined in their own block, i.e. functions are not nested within functions, as could be the case in languages such as Pascal/Modula-2. A function name is of storage class **extern** and is thus global to all functions found after it in the same file and indeed in other files which are to be linked with it. This means that you must make function names unique and not declare external variables of the same name.

scanf()

```
scanf("%lf",&Number_1)
                ;
```

It is worth noting here that the library function `scanf()` always requires the address of variables for reading values into those variables. For this reason the address operator **&** must be used to provide the address of the variable `Number_1`.

It would be a good idea to look up the `scanf` function call in your manual. It is in the `stdio` library.

Language-specific features

C as a block-structured language
One point worth raising here is the nature of C as a block-structured language. Clearly C can be described as 'procedural' and thus defines blocks which are local to a particular function. However, since functions cannot be defined within functions, the scoping of variables is somewhat simpler than that which is encountered in languages such as Pascal, Modula-2 and ADA. We will investigate further these scoping rules and how modularity and encapsulation can be achieved in C, both features being central to modern program design.

Compound statements
In C, a function body always contains a compound statement and the language allows the definition of a variable to exist anywhere that a compound statement begins. Care must be taken with this as presence of variables of the same name already defined in the function will lead to a compiler error. Remember that a parameter is a local variable, so the same applies to a conflict with the parameter name, e.g. in

```
func(int a, int b, int c)
{
       int a;
```

the local variable a is redefined and a compiler error results.

Exercises on functions

3.1   Write a function which accepts an integer, a real number and a character as parameters and prints them out in order lowest to highest. Clearly, for the character the ASCII value is used.

3.2   Write a C program which displays as a menu a choice of the drinks whiskey, gin, coke, brandy. Your program should allow the user to select a drink, input the number of bottles of drink of that type required and calculate the cost of buying those bottles. Here the price of whiskey is £12.20 per bottle, gin £8.50 per bottle, coke £0.72 per bottle and brandy £12.12 per bottle. Users should be allowed to choose more than one type of drink and the total charge for the whole purchase is to be calculated and displayed when a user indicates that no further drinks are desired.

Modular programming in C

The previous section introduced the fact that variables have scope, which is determined by where they are defined in a file. A variable can be local to a compound statement within a function, local to a function or defined outside a function and global to all the functions after it has been defined. In reality, programmers must often work in large teams on large software projects, sometimes taking years with staff leaving and new staff arriving during the project. Since C is a much used industrial/commercial language it is important that the language supports some degree of modularity so that teams can work effectively but independently in writing and testing different but related parts of a software system.

The problem.

Let us now explore some of the issues arising by considering the following problem:

> The original calculator program is to be used and extended so that other functions can be used – these being square root, square and reciprocal (1/x). The original menu is simply to provide another option which calls another menu of further calculator functions. These further functions should be able to act on a newly input number, on the result of the last calculation (i.e. from the +, −, *, /, x2, 1/x, root x) or on the current memory contents.
>
> Different programmers are to write these new routines, one writing the new menu system, the other writing the new calculator functions.
>
> At a programmers' meeting, the original programmer plus the two new programmers must sketch out their modular design so that each can go away and work independently on implementing their routines.
>
> Show the changes that are required to the original calculator program and show how the software can be structured to allow modular development of code. The details of function implementation are **not** required.

Modular design allows each programmer to identify one or more groups of related functions and to implement these independently.

A solution

Let us now take a look at how the software can be structured: The following is a possible suggestion, remember that with a problem of any complexity there are many solutions. One way forward would have been to simply extend the original calculator program, but it was decided that three programmers would work in parallel on this project.

The project is to be divided into three areas – changes to the original program, the menu system and the new calculator functions. It makes sense to create three sets of functions in different files as there are three programmers involved. These functions can then be used to extend the calculator program and may be later reused in other functions or programs.

The program `main()` and amended original calculator functions will be implemented in file **calc.c**.

The new menu functions will be implemented in file `menu.c`.
The new calculator functions will be implemented in file `funcs.c`.

Changes to the original calculator program to create `calc.c`
These changes are to be made by the first programmer.

The functions `display_menu()` and `process_nums()` are updated to allow for the new functionality.

```
#include "menu.h"
    .

    .

double result, memory;

void display_menu(void)
{

        .

        .

        printf("F    for further functions\n");

        .

        .

}




char process_nums()
{
        extern double result, memory;

        .

        .

        switch(Option){

        .

        .

                        case 'F' :{
                                extra_show_menu();
                                extra_process_menu();
                                break;
                                }

        .

        .

}
```

Let us now look at the above changes to the original calculator program.

Function changes

```
printf("F   for further functions\n");
```
and
```
case 'F' :{

            extra_show_menu();

            extra_process_menu();

            break;

            }
```

The first change involves adding a new option to the display_menu() function and correspondingly then altering process_nums() to include the new calls extra_show_menu() and extra_process_menu().

Include file

```
#include "menu.h"
```

Now that we have used the new functions extra_show_menu() and extra_process_menu() we therefore need to know at least the function prototypes. Since this is part of the menu system, we can hold the prototypes in an include file (also known as a header file) called **menu.h.** This can now be included at the top of file calc.c using the preprocessor command:

```
#include "menu.h"
```

The quotes tell the compiler to look for the file in the current working directory. If located elsewhere, then a full path name must be given. Remember if <menu.h> is written then the compiler will look in the standard place which is dependent upon your implementation, that is the place where all the standard include files are found such as <stdio.h>.

The header file menu.h is used in a similar way to the definition module in Modula-2. The functions prototyped in menu.h are implemented in the file menu.c.

External variables

```
double result, memory;
```

The next change involves the fact that the new calculator functions require access to the variables result and memory currently found locally in the function do_sum().

These variables are now to be made global and, to achieve this, they are defined in the file calc.c, before the function process_nums(). These variables are now of the external storage class. The reason that they were not placed at the top of the file is that in the file calc.c only the function process_nums() requires them, so they are defined as late as possible to limit scope within the file. The external variables cannot be seen in functions before their definition, but are global to everything found after this.

Those variables which are still referenced in the function `do_sum()` should now be changed. Since they are external variables they are now written as **`extern double result, memory;`** This makes sure that the external variables are used even if defined after this function. It is also worth remembering that local variables of the same name will mask the external variables within the function, so beware!

Creating `calc.h`

```
                extern double result, memory;
                double get_number(void);
```
The header file `calc.h` contains the above two lines.

Since the external variables `result` and `memory` are to be made available to functions in other files, an include file can be created (`calc.h`) which contains the line **`extern double result, memory;`** This makes sure that other files which include `calc.h` have available the external variables `result` and `memory` from `calc.c`.

It is worth noting that by using the keyword `extern` this becomes a **declaration** and does not provide storage. An external variable must be **defined** (i.e. storage allocated) only once and this is done in file `calc.c`.

The function `get_number()` is also to be used in the menu functions and so the prototype for this function is included in the file `calc.h` as **`double get_number(void);`** The function is implemented in the corresponding file `calc.c`.

This allows the menu programmer to use the function in the correct way and to have parameter types and return types checked by the compiler. The menu programmer does not have to know anything about the way the function is implemented. It is also worth mentioning that since this is a sort of function synopsis, it is usual to include a description of the function – what it does, a description of parameters and expected return values and their meanings, along with the prototype.

Creation of `funcs.c`

```c
double square(double Number)
{
            /* An example implementation */
        return(Number * Number);
}


double squareroot(double Number)
{
/* implementation */
}


double reciprocal(double Number)
{
/* implementation */
}
```

funcs.c and funcs.h are created by the second programmer. Let us look at the structure of the above code for funcs.c.

The functions

The functions square(), square root() and reciprocal() each take an argument of type double. When these functions are called then either the result of last arithmetic calculation (i.e. from the +, -, *, /, x^2, $1/x$, root x) or the current memory contents can be passed in as copies since these functions do not need to directly alter the current result and memory values held in the external variables.

The functions square(), squareroot() and reciprocal() return the result of their calculation to their calling environment in extra_do_sum().

Creating funcs.h

This file needs to contain the function prototypes of the functions in funcs.c so that they can be included in the menu file, menu.c. This will also serve to instruct the menu programmer on how to use the functions and what to expect as return values. The compiler can also then check typing when the functions are called.

The contents of funcs.h are as follows:

```
double square(double);
double square root(double);
double reciprocal(double);
```

Creating menu.c

```
#include "calc.h"
#include "funcs.h"

/* Function prototype */
double extra_do_sum(double);

void extra_show_menu(void)
{
        printf("T to act on last result\n");
        printf("M to act on stored memory\n");
        printf("N to input a new number\n");
}

char extra_process_menu(void)
{
        extern double result;
        char funcoption;

        while((funcoption = getchar()) == '\n');
```

```
        switch(funcoption)
        {
         case 'T' : {
                 result = extra_do_sum(result);
                 break;
                         }
         case 'M' : {
                 result = extra_do_sum(memory);
                 break;
                         }
         case 'N' : {
                 result = extra_do_sum(get_number());
                 break;
                         }
         default : printf("Option not recognised");
         }


}

static double extra_do_sum(double input)
{
        char inchar;

        printf("Q for square root\n");
        .

        .

        .
        while((input = getchar()) == '\n');
        switch(inchar)
        {
        case 'Q' :{
                return(square(input));
                break;
                         }
        .

        .


        /* In this function calls are made to
          the extra functions - square(),
            square root() and reciprocal() */
}
```

menu c. and menu.h are created by the third programmer. Let us examine the above structure of menu.c.

Include files

```
#include "calc.h"
#include "funcs.h"
```

The menu functions require access to the external variables `result` and `memory` from `file.c` and to use the functions created in `funcs.c`.

Function `extra_process_menu()`

```
char extra_process_menu(void)
{
    extern double result, memory;
```

This function has to store the results returned from the various calculations (square, square root, reciprocal) in the external `result`. It must therefore contain the extern declaration for `result`. The result is captured by statements such as **`result = extra_do_sum(memory)`;** Notice how memory or result are passed as a parameter to `extra_do_sum()`; this makes explicit the fact that only a copy of these external variables is needed by this function.

Creating `menu.h`

In order to make the functions `extra_process_menu()` and `extra_do_sum()` available for use in functions defined in other files, we need to make them available as function prototypes in `menu.h`. Functions are by default of the external storage class (global). This is included by the file `calc.c`.

The following shows the contents of `menu.h`:

```
void extra_show_menu(void);
void extra_process_menu(void);
```

Language-specific features

Static storage class

One feature that is found in C is that external variables can be defined to be of storage class `static`,. e.g.

```
static int number;
```

which is defined outside of functions. This results in global storage which is confined to the file in which it is defined and gives an extra level of scope restriction. If you have met the concept of abstract data types implemented in languages such as Modula-2, then you will see how this could be used to hold storage accessed by a set of service routines which are held together in one file.

Further, although less commonly encountered, functions can be defined as `static`, which then limits visiblity of the function to the rest of the file within which it is defined, e.g.

```
static int func(int a, char b)
{
etc...
```

Such an example is to be found in `menu.c`. The function `static double extra_do_sum(char)` is only used by functions in the file `menu.c` and its visibility or scope can thus be limited to this file.

Summary for C functions

- The basic function structure is:
  ```
  return_type function_name( parameter declarations, if used)
  {
  declarations;

  statements;
  }
  ```
- Function prototypes are a way of declaring a function's parameter number, type and the return type, so that the compiler can check these types in function calls before the function is fully defined, i.e. implemented (either in the same file or in another file).
- Function names are 'external', i.e. global to everything after the definition and across files unless made `static` in which case function scope is limited to the same file and after the definition of the function.
- The type `void` is used to indicate either that the function expects no parameters or that it does not return a value.
- Function parameter passing is always by value, i.e. a copy from the calling environment. The parameter is treated as a local variable inside the function.
- Functions cannot be nested.
- Variables defined inside a function are local, of the storage class 'automatic' and uninitialized and they exist only for the duration of the function call unless explicitly made storage class `static`.
- Variables of the external storage class defined outside of functions are global from the point of definition. External variables must be defined once and once only.
- The `extern` declaration allows external variables to be used before the point of definition in the same file or to use external variables from another file.
- Include files can be used to provide function prototypes and extern declarations to other files, using these functions and external variables.

Exercises on modular programming

3.3 Write a group of functions which implement the following functionality:
(a) Checks whether a supplied character is upper-case alphabetic,
returning one if true, zero otherwise.
(b) Checks whether a supplied character is a vowel, returning one if
true, zero otherwise. Character can be upper or lower case.
(c) Checks whether a supplied character is a consonant, returning one
if true and zero otherwise.
These functions are to be made available for use by other programmers. Show how you would provide these functions and yet hide the
details of their implementation.

3.4 Present by way of discussion how features of the C language allow a
programmer to control the visiblity of functions and variables.

Chapter 4

Arrays and pointers in C

OBJECTIVES

On completion of this chapter you will be able to:

☐ declare, initialize and access one- and two-dimensional arrays;

☐ pass and manipulate arrays as parameters;

☐ use pointers with the address and dereferencing operator;

☐ explain how pointers and arrays are related;

☐ use pointer arithmetic;

☐ achieve pass by reference.

So far you will have had little awareness of pointers in C, though you have in fact been using them. However, the introduction of arrays means that there is a need for you to begin to understand how C uses pointers, because arrays and pointers are strongly linked. We will assume you know about arrays and we will begin with a simple example program which shows you how to declare, initialize and modify them in C. The subsequent examples will concentrate on the interrelationship of arrays with pointers. Finally, some of the more complex and powerful features of pointers will be explored through an examination of pointer arithmetic and how pointers to pointers can be used in C programs will be discussed.

A simple example involving a recap on using arrays

This section will present a problem which is most naturally solved using arrays and array manipulation.

Write a program that offers a customer a menu choice of groceries which can be purchased (sugar, bread, salt, butter, milk) or the option to quit the program. The customer can select an item and is asked the quantity required. The customer can purchase any number of items in any order and even repeat buy a particular item. When the customer chooses to

quit, an itemized bill is produced showing the quantity of each item pur-
chased and the amount owed. Prices are to be set at: sugar 54p, bread
76p, salt 24p, butter 59p and milk 32p.

Structured-English solution

Initialize the StockItem, ItemCount and Price arrays
Display a menu
Get choice of item
While item choice obtained is not quit
       Get quantity of item
       Calculate and add cost to bill
       Update item count
       Display menu
End
Display itemized bill

The program

```c
#include <stdio.h>
#define NumOfItems 6          /* constant used for sizing arrays */


main()
{
                        /* function prototypes */
        void DisplayMenu(char Items[NumOfItems][10]);
        int GetChoice(void);
        int GetQuantity(void);
        void UpdateItemCount(int, int,int);
        void DisplayDetails(char,int,float, float);

        /* variables for main() */
        int Reply;       /* holds index of item chosen */
        int Quantity;    /* holds required number of chosen item */

                    /* declare and setup arrays */
        char StockItems[NumOfItems][10] = {"Sugar", "Bread", "Salt",
                                "Butter", "Milk", "Quit"};

        int   ItemCount[NumOfItems - 1] = { 0,0,0,0,0};

        float Price[NumOfItems - 1] = {0.54, 0.76, 0.24, 0.59, 0.32};

        float ShoppingBill = 0.0;

                    /* start of main program */
```

```
        DisplayMenu(StockItems);        /* pass array as parameter */
        while ((Reply = GetChoice()) != NumOfItems)
        {
            ShoppingBill = ShoppingBill + (Quantity = GetQuantity())
                        * Price[Reply - 1];
                                /* array modified in function */
            UpdateItemCount(ItemCount, Quantity, Reply);
        DisplayMenu(StockItems);
        }
        DisplayDetails(StockItems, ItemCount, Price, ShoppingBill);
        printf("\n\nHave a nice day.\n\n");
        return(0);
} /* end of main() */

void DisplayMenu(char Items[NumOfItems][10])
{
        int Count;      /* loop control variable */

        printf("\n\nWhich item do you wish to purchase?");
        for (Count = 0; Count < NumOfItems; Count++)
        {
                printf("\n\n\t\t%d %s",(Count + 1),Items[Count]);
                            /* Note usage of array here */
        }
        printf("\n\n");
}


int GetChoice(void)
{
        int Reply;

        do
        {
                printf("Select an item [1,2,3,4,5,6] ..>");
                scanf("%d", &Reply);
        }
        while ((Reply < 1) || (Reply > NumOfItems));
        return(Reply);
}


int GetQuantity(void)
{
        int Number;

        do
```

```
      {
        printf("\nWhat quantity of this item do you require ..>");
        scanf("%d", &Number);
      }
      while (Number < 1);
      return(Number);
}


void UpdateItemCount(int Totals[NumOfItems], int Quantity, int Index)
{
                    /* array parameter permanently modified here */
      Totals[Index - 1] += Quantity;
}


void DisplayDetails(char StockItems[NumOfItems][10], int ItemCount[],
                    float Prices[], float Bill)
{
      int Count;              /* loop control variable */

      for (Count = 0; Count < NumOfItems - 1; Count++)
      {
            if (ItemCount[Count] > 0)
            {
                  printf("\n\t%3d \t%s\t@ %6.2f = %6.2f",
                        ItemCount[Count], StockItems[Count],
                        Prices[Count], ItemCount[Count] *
                        Prices[Count]);
            }
      }
      printf("\n\nThe total for this list is\t  %6.2f\n\n", Bill);
}
```

Let us now examine the structure of the above program:

Declaring arrays

```
          char   StockItems[NumOfItems][10];
          int    ItemCount[NumOfItems - 1];
          float  Price[NumOfItems - 1];
```

This example uses integer, float and character arrays of both one and two dimensions, and then demonstrates how to initialize arrays when they are declared. It also shows how to manipulate arrays and pass them as parameters to functions, though you should note that in one function (UpdateItemCount()) an array parameter is modified and that change is permanent!

There are several ways in which arrays in C differ from arrays in other languages and the first of these is that you are not allowed to specify the lower bound, this is always zero (0). Thus when you declare an integer array which requires ten elements you should declare it as follows:

```
int ArrayTen[10];
```

The point to remember is that the array is indexed from 0 to 9 in this case. Of course if you want ten elements and you wish to access them using the indices 1...10 then you can declare the array to be:

```
int ArrayTen[11];
```

and ignore the first element − `ArrayTen[0]`. However, you do so at your peril (pointers and addresses form part of this danger as you will see later in this chapter).

Another point that you should know about arrays is that their dimensions MUST be set at compile time, i.e. C does not support dynamic array declaration through the use of variable array dimensions. Thus, when you declare an array the compiler should be able to calculate its size, which means that the bounds given should be either constants, literal constants or constant expressions, e.g.

```
#define Maximum 25

main()
{
     int Numbers [Maximum];          /* uses a constant */
     float Sums [Maximum * 2];/* uses a constant expression */
     char Letters[51];               /* uses a literal value */
     .

     .

}
```

When an array of two dimensions is declared,then the rightmost dimension will always be the number of columns, e.g.

```
int Numbers[25];
/* single dimension array of 25 elements */
int MoreNumbers[5][25];
       /* two dimension array, 5 rows and 25 columns */
```

Initializing arrays

```
char StockItems[NumOfItems][10] = {"Sugar", "Bread", "Salt",
                                "Butter", "Milk", "Quit"};
int    ItemCount[NumOfItems − 1] = { 0,0,0,0,0};
float Price[NumOfItems − 1]    = {0.54, 0.76, 0.24, 0.59, 0.32};
```

The program illustrates both the declaration and initialization of integer, float and character arrays. With regard to the integer and float examples there is little to say except that:

- the initialization values must be enclosed by {};
- each value should be separated by a comma;
- it is sensible to make the values of the same type as the array (though coercion can be applied);
- it is sensible to ensure that the number of initializers matches the number of elements of the array, though if there are too few they will be accepted and the array will comprise initialized elements and the remainder will be initialized as if of the `static` storage class, i.e. to zeros. Where there are too many initialization values the compiler will complain.

One feature of C is that if the dimensions of the array are omitted in the declaration then the compiler will compute the size of the array from the number of initializing items, e.g.

> Note that a string can be treated as a `null` (\0) terminated array of characters.

```
char items[][10] = {"sugar", "salt", "bread"};
```

will produce an array of three string items. Notice that the only dimension which can be omitted is the row dimension for automatic sizing.

Close examination of the character array reveals several unusual aspects. For example, when the two-dimensional array `StockItems` is initialized the values are actually a series of strings enclosed in "" and there are as many of these strings as there are rows in the array. Equally, the way in which this array is used is somewhat different in that, though it is declared as a two-dimensional array, it is used as though it were a one-dimensional array. In the function `DisplayMenu()` the values of the array are accessed as `Items[Count]`, i.e. as a one-dimensional array and not as `Items[Count][InnerCount]`, i.e. a two-dimensional array. This arises because each item name is accessed as a row and so only the row is used.

The more usual declaration and initilization of multiple-dimension arrays of the base data types is illustrated below:

```
# define Rows 3
# define Columns 5

        int Table[Rows][Columns] =    { {  1,  2,  3,  4, 5},
                                        {  6,  7,  8,  9,10},
                                        { 11,12,13,14,15,}
                                        };
```

Notice that the values used to the initialize the elements of each row are themselves contained within a pair of {} and separated by commas. Also notice that each matched pair of {} are themselves separated by commas.

There is no syntactic need to place each set of initializers on separate lines, as in the example above, but it is an aid to the readability of the code and as such is to be recommended as good practice.

For arrays of three dimensions the principle is the same, e.g.

```
#define Rows 2
#define Columns 3
#define Depth 5

              int Cube [Rows][Columns][Depth] =
                   {         { {  1,  2,  3,  4, 5},
                             {  6,  7,  8,  9,10},
                             { 11,12,13,14,15,}
                             },
                             { { 0, 0, 0, 0, 0},
                             { 1, 1, 1, 1, 1},
                             { 2, 2, 2, 2, 2}
                             }
                   };
```

Passing arrays as parameters

```
DisplayMenu (StockItems);
```

If you look at the function calls where an array is passed as a parameter, a perfectly valid action, you will notice that all that is given is the name of the array and this is a common way of passing arrays as parameters in many languages. There is a very important fact to remember about this action in C; the name of an array is a substitute for the address of the first element of that array. As you will see, this is used in a variety of ways within C.

Array parameters are passed by address

```
UpdateItemCount (ItemCount, Quantity, Reply);
```

It should be noted that a copy of the whole array passed as the parameter is not possible as the compiler always passes the address of the first element

Pursuing the same theme of unusal facets of the program, there is an example of an array being passed as a parameter to a function and the clear intention of that function is to modify an element of that array – ItemCount. Furthermore that modification is permanent since the result is used later in the program. How can this be if C only supports pass by value parameters?

Recall that, when the function is called, the parameter given is the array name and you have just learned that this is actually the address of the first element in the array. Consequently, references to elements of the array within the function are actually addressing the elements of the actual array and not some copy. In this way C provides a generalized route for achieving parameter passing by reference, i.e. rather than pass the value of a parameter, pass its address!

One further point to bring out is the need to manipulate the values of variables used to index the arrays. Remember that in C all arrays have a lower bound of zero and so most of the index variables are initialized to zero. However, when interacting with the user it is not zero but the value 'one' which 'naturally' forms the first of a sequence. As a result you will notice the variables like `Count` in `DisplayMenu()` are used to access the array but are displayed with their current value plus one for creating the menu list. Similiarly in the function `UpdateItemCount()` the parameter `Index`, which is the user's choice, is used with one deducted from its value to map the user view of things to that of C code.

Exercises on arrays

4.1 Write a program that reads in a list of ten integers and then prints them out in reverse order.

4.2 Write a program that prompts the user for, and reads in, an array of ten integers and the direction (ascending or descending). Your program should then sort the integers into the given order, i.e. ascending or descending order. Use functions to both read in the data and do the sorting. You may choose any suitable sort method.

A simple introduction to pointers

Pointers are simply variables which can hold the address of an object. Pointers form a major part of both the power and flexibility of C, more so than most other languages. You can declare pointers which 'point' to items of any of the base types (and consequently to any of the data structures which can be built up from these types).

Write a simple program which illustrates how to declare a pointer, make it point at something and then modify the contents of that item. Then go on to show a program which uses pointers to achieve a call by reference parameter passing to a function.

The program

```
/***************************************************/
/*                                                 */
/* Simple program to illustrate that a pointer     */
/* holds an address. Whatever it points to it only */
/* contains an address. By following that address  */
/* you can modify the contents held at that address*/
/*                                                 */
/***************************************************/
```

```
#include <stdio.h>

main()
{
        char CharVar = 'z';   /* character variable */
        char *CharPtr;        /* pointer to a char variable */

                       /* start of main program */

        CharPtr = &CharVar;   /* pointer points to variable */
        printf("\nCharVar is %c, pointer value is %u, contents ",
                                     CharVar, CharPtr);
        printf("of thing CharPtr points to is %c\n",*CharPtr);

        CharVar = 'A';        /* modify the character variable */
        printf("\nCharVar is %c, pointer value is %u, contents ",
                                     CharVar, CharPtr);
        printf("of thing CharPtr points to is %c\n",*CharPtr);

        *CharPtr = 'B';       /* modify the thing the pointer */
                              /* points to */
        printf("\nCharVar is %c, pointer value is %u, contents ",
                                     CharVar, CharPtr);
        printf("of thing CharPtr points to is %c\n",*CharPtr);
                              /* preincrement value of thing */
                              /* pointer points to.          */
        ++*CharPtr;
        printf("\nCharVar is %c, pointer value is %u, contents ",
                                     CharVar, CharPtr);
        printf("of thing CharPtr points to is %c\n",*CharPtr);
        return(0);
        }
```

Let us now take a look at the features of this program.

Declaring pointers

char *CharPtr;

It cannot be emphasized too strongly that declaring a pointer only gets you a piece of memory big enough to hold an address. This is so whether the pointer is a pointer to an int, a float, a char or some very large data structure which requires kilobytes of storage. A pointer only holds the address of the thing it points at. Thus the declaration informs the compiler that CharPtr is a pointer, it requires as much memory as is needed to hold an address and it can be used to 'point to' things whose data type is char. So this is a pointer to items of the type `char` only, i.e. it is not a pointer to any and everything. The `*` in front of the pointer identifier informs the compiler that this is a pointer. A pointer is not initialized when it is declared (though you can arrange this) and in order for it to be useful you have to make it point to something of the correct type.

Since our example contains a pointer to `char`, it might be tempting to assign a character value to that pointer.

```
CharPtr = 'a';
```

This would be invalid; remember that a pointer can only hold an address.

Assigning to a pointer

CharPtr = &CharVar;

The program shows how to bring the pointer into use by using the address operator `&`. Here the address operator returns a pointer to the variable `CharVar` and this is assigned to `CharPtr`.

Accessing variables through the pointer

printf("\n\nCharVar is %c contents of thing CharPtr points to %c\n\n",

CharVar, *CharPtr);

Having given a value to the pointer, how do you use it, and. what is more to the point. how do you distinguish between the address itself and the contents of that address? Once again C has an operator which assists you here, the dereferencing operator `*`. To use the address in a pointer, use the pointer name, to use the value contained in the address held by the pointer use `*pointer name`.

Changing variable contents using the pointer

*CharPtr = 'B';

Now that you can get at the value held at the address contained within the pointer, it should be obvious that not only can you retrieve it but also you can change it. In the same way that you can assign an address to a pointer you can assign a value to the address pointed to by that pointer, although, of course, such a value should be of the appropriate type. Thus in the example program this is shown quite simply in the above statement.

The same could have been achieved in a more complex manner as:

```
++*CharPtr
```

This latter example uses the pre-increment operator to add one to the value held at the address pointed to by the pointer. The effect of this is make the letter 'A' into a 'B'. This mixture of pointers and pre/post-increment/decrement operators is very common and you need to be quite clear what you intend when you use them. A fuller description of this is given in the section on language-specific features.

Pointers and call-by-reference parameter passing

In the earlier section on arrays there was an example of some code in which an array was passed into a function and the contents of that array were permanently changed. It was explained that this came about because the array name was used as the actual parameter and that in C this is really the address of the array, thus making the array a pass-by-reference parameter. Now that you have the pointer and the address operator, it is time to show how to achieve pass-by-reference parameters for things other than arrays. Here is a simple program which illustrates this.

The program

```c
/*****************************************************/
/*                                                   */
/* Simple program to demonstrate pointers, the       */
/* address operator and pass by reference parameter*/
/* passing in C                                      */
/*                                                   */
/*****************************************************/

#include <stdio.h>

main()
{
                  /* function prototypes */
     float GetCost(int *Quantity, float *Price);

     int Number = 0;
     float Charge = 0.0;
     float TotalCost = 0.0;

     printf("\n\nBefore call Number is %d, Charge is %6.2f "
          "TotalCost is %6.2f\n\n", Number, Charge,
                                        TotalCost);

     /* call function and pass addresses of variables */

     TotalCost = GetCost(&Number, &Charge);
     printf("\n\nAfter call Number is %d, Charge is %6.2f "
          "TotalCost is %6.2f\n\n", Number, Charge,
                                        TotalCost);
     return(0);

}
```

```
float GetCost(int *Quantity, float *Price)
{
     *Quantity = 5;              /* modify contents of addresses */
     *Price = 1.25;             /* pointed to by pointers        */
     return(*Quantity * *Price); /* context determines use       */
}                                /* of the '*', pointer or       */
                                 /* multiplication.              */
```

Let us look at the features shown in this program.

Pointer and address operators

float GetCost(int *Quantity, float *Price);

TotalCost = GetCost(&Number, &Charge);

The essence of this program is the use of the pointer operator * both in the GetCost() function prototype and in the body of that function, and also the use of the address operator & with both the actual parameters passed in the call to GetCost() from the function main(). The * operator against a formal parameter in the function prototype tells the compiler to expect a pointer to the data type (that is an address of the data type) for that parameter and not a value of that data type. Thus in the above example the function GetCost() is declared as expecting two parameters, the first a pointer to an int and the second a pointer to a float.

In order to match the formal parameters, any call to GetCost() must give two pointers (addresses), the first to an int and the second to a float, as the actual parameters. This is done through the address operator & which takes an item and returns the address of it. As a result the function GetCost() receives two pointers for its actual parameters and these contain the addresses of the variables in the calling function main(). You already know how to access the contents of the address that a pointer points to and so, using the * operator, the function GetCost() can both access and modify the contents of the variables Number and Charge found in the calling function main().

This is how C allows call-by-reference parameter passing.

Exercises on pointers

4.3 Rewrite the program that you wrote for Exercise 4.2, but do not use array subscripts; use pointers only.

4.4 Write a function that accepts two English words as strings parameters and returns the value one if they are the same, zero otherwise. You may NOT use the standard C libraries <string.h>.

Pointer arithmetic in C

This section outlines some very powerful language specific features of C – pointer arithmetic and strings.

You may have noticed that some of the examples containing pointers have used the increment or decrement operators in association with those pointers. Perhaps you have asked yourself the question how it is that the same operation appears to achieve the correct result with different types. i.e. incrementing a pointer to `int` moves you on to the next `int` and incrementing a pointer to `float` moves you on to the next `float`. The answer lies in the fact that a pointer variable is a pointer to a type and the type is used to work out what the effect of incrementing or decrementing a pointer will be. This also holds for pointers to data structures, as you will see later.

C allows you to add or subtract integral amounts to pointers and this can be used not only to move a pointer along the elements of an array but also to determine the difference between two pointers to the same array. Here the difference will be the number of elements between the pointers, e.g.

```
/******************************************* */
/*                                          */
/* Demonstration of determining and printing */
/* the difference between two pointers to    */
/* the same array                            */
/*                                          */
/******************************************* */

#include <stdio.h>

main()
{
        int Numbers[10] = { 1, 2, 3, 4, 5,
                              6, 7, 8, 9, 10 };
        int *Ptr1, *Ptr2;

        for (Ptr1 = Numbers, Ptr2 = Numbers;
                            Ptr1 < &Numbers[10]; Ptr1++)
        {
                printf("\nIteration %d Ptr1 - Ptr2 = %ld",
                        *Ptr1,(long)(Ptr1 - Ptr2));
        }
        printf("\n\nProgram terminates here.\n\n");
        return(0);
}
```

Notice once again that the name of the array `Numbers` is used to generate a pointer which is used by both `Ptr1` and `Ptr2`.

The example does not show this, but the difference between two pointers can of course be negative and this shows that the integral value must be signed. This can be used to great effect in applications such as searching and comparison.

In the example program above we have used the format specifier `%ld` to print the integral difference between two pointers. This is because implementations of the type for this difference vary. Consequently, we have chosen the type `long int` which encompasses all possibilities and 'cast' the result into this type. Your own implementation may work perfectly well just using `int` specifiers.

Some interesting extensions to pointers

The typing restrictions in C indicate that a pointer to type `int` cannot be made to point to an object of type `float` (or indeed any other type). Unlike expressions which use mixed type values there is no implicit coercion of pointers from one type to another, which is excellent news from a software engineering viewpoint. However, there are a number of instances where this is an extremely limiting restriction. One such example you will meet is the dynamic allocation of memory. Here a function (`malloc()`) is called to obtain a piece of memory big enough to hold an object of a specified type and it returns a pointer to the memory that it grabs. So we are using a single function to get memory for all data types and it should return a pointer to the data type it has just got memory for. However, the typing restriction would mean that each data type would need its own function and that user-defined types would need to create their own dynamic memory allocation functions.

C provides a route around this problem through the `void` pointer. A pointer of this type can have the value of any other pointer assigned to it and equally its value can be assigned to any other pointer. Thus the memory allocation function returns a value of type pointer to `void` and this value is then 'cast' into a pointer to the requisite data type (examples of this can be found in the Chapter 6).

Null pointer

In languages such as Modula-2 and Pascal there is an explicit `NULL` value for use with pointers, particularly where list processing is involved. Its purpose is to indicate that any pointer having that value explicitly points to no object. In C you need to construct such a value yourself. In essence it is the integral constant 0 or a void pointer to this value, e.g.

```
const int Null = 0;
```

```
return( (void *) 0);
```

Addressing memory using known locations

You, the programmer, can assign the value 0 to a pointer (the null pointer) or the value of another pointer to a pointer. If you have a machine which has memory-mapped i/o and you wish by pass the operating system routines for reading and writing then you will need to address the relevant memory locations directly. How you can do this in C involves the use of pointers and casting. Assume that you need to extract the value of memory location 128, here is one way to achieve that:

```
int *IOport;
int PortValue;


IOport = (int *) 128; /* cast the address into a pointer to int */


PortValue = *Ioport; /* get the value held in the thing pointed to */
```

This is yet another indication of how closely C is aligned with the machine hardware. Obviously this facility allows you to perform many actions which are normally done using assembler in the higher-level language. C has other operators to make those actions much easier.

Character handling

See Appendix E on the standard C library for details on the string libraries.

As a systems programming language C needs to be able to cope with character-based i/o, both in the form of streams of bytes and as strings. If you recall information from the early chapters where it was indicated that C was a very small language and as such it did not directly support any form of i/o, then you should question the ability of C to perform character-based processing. No doubt, you also recall that C uses libraries for i/o, in particular stdio.h, and it also has a standard library included as string.h for assisting in processing strings (which are null (\0) terminated arrays of characters). Here is an example program which demonstrates how to read in an array of characters and then how to write them out.

```
#include <stdio.h>

#define LineLength 80
main()
{
                /* Function prototypes, note the declaration of */
                /* the array params, merely an array of ints!   */
        void ReadLine(int Line[], int Length);
        void PrintLine(int Line[]);

        int Line[LineLength + 1]; /* extra char for Null terminator */
        int *CharPtr;
```

```
        printf("\n\nEnter your characters:\n\n>");
        ReadLine(Line, LineLength);
        printf("\n\nYou entered the following characters:\n\n");
        PrintLine(Line);
        return(0);
}


void ReadLine(int Line[], int Length)
{                       /* Length is array size, so function more
            general in operation */
        int *CharPtr = Line;
        int Count = 0;

        while ( (Count++ < Length) &&    /* one less than actual
                            array size so space for */
            ((*CharPtr = getchar()) != '\n'))   /* line
                                                terminator */
        {
            CharPtr++;
        }
        *CharPtr = '\0';    /* put the null terminator on the     */
                    /* string of characters just read in */

}


void PrintLine(int Line[])
{
        int *CharPtr = Line;

        while (*CharPtr != '\0')   /* look for string terminator */
        {
            putchar(*CharPtr++); /* complement to getchar, held */
        }                        /* in the include file stdio.h */
        printf("\n\nEnd of output!\n\n");

}
```

This program introduces several variations on things you have previously seen. The first and most important is the change in the array parameter description in the functions and in stating their prototypes. Rather than explicitly stating that the parameter is an array of LineLength integers, the description indicates only that the parameter is an array of integers. If you remember open array parameters in Modula-2 or conformant arrays in Pascal, then this is something very similar. In effect it means that the function expects only an array of integers, i.e. a pointer, of course. It is up to you to ensure that the array bounds are not transgressed. Hence, in the function ReadLine() the second parameter is used to indicate the size of the array passed as the first parameter. C will quite happily allow you to put values in the objects pointed by a pointer until you run up against some contravention of the typing rules, run out of memory for your process or attempt to access some restricted area of memory. Be warned!

A second feature of the program is the rather strange size of the array `Line` in the main function. It is not `LineLength` but `LineLength + 1`. Why should this be? The difference between a character and a string is that a string is zero or more characters (enclosed in matching double quotes) and terminated by a null character or the escape sequence `\0`, i.e. the length of a string is $N + 1$ characters. In the processing of the input the series of characters read in is stored in the array and this is then terminated by hand with a `\0`. This is then used to indicate the end of the output when the array is printed. Note that when a string is created by the system, e.g. a call to `scanf` with a `%s` specifier, or when a literal string is embedded in a program, the system automatically places the `null` terminator at the end of the string. However, when you explicitly create a string, character by character, as in the example program, you must put in the terminator at the end of the string.

Notice the use made of pointers and the increment operator for accessing the array, this is very typical of C array processing. A new function was introduced in the `PrintLine()` function, this was `putchar()`. As might be guessed it is the complement to `getchar()` and it prints out its integer argument on the standard output, usually the VDU or monitor. Actually both `getchar()` and `putchar()` hide some lower-level functions which are more general i/o routines. These will be brought forward when we discuss file-based i/o.

Strings in C

A string is an array of `char` terminated by the `null` character (`\0`). When the compiler creates a string this is also an array of `char` terminated by the `null` character, for example the literal string:

```
"Hello World"
```

is really 12 characters long, the 11 you can see, including the space, and the unseen `null` character. In fact a literal string is both its own value and a pointer to itself since the literal is an array of `char` terminated by the `null` and the only way to get at it is to use it.

Pointers and increment/decrement operators

You should by now have recognized the strong interaction between pointers and arrays. Many of the examples you have met have used pointers to access arrays and also used the increment or decrement operators on those pointers to enable sequential access. One area of difficulty which arises from using these operators with pointers is that of intention, for example what does the following code fragment actually do?

```
#define Length 25

float Totals[Length];
float *TotalPtr = Totals;

while (TotalPtr < &Totals[Length])
{
        *(TotalPtr++) = 0.0;
}
```

The obvious answer is that it sets all the elements of the array `Totals` to zero, but how does it do that and in particular what is the importance of the expression `*(TotalPtr++)`? In words, the aim is to set the value of the element of the array pointed to by `TotalPtr` to 0.0 and then to move the pointer onto the next element. This is done until the pointer points to the element one above the upper bound. Does the code match these words?

The answer is yes, because we have used the post-increment operator to be applied to the pointer, and we dereference (get the value of the object pointed at) first. Why did we need the parentheses? Actually, we didn't need them, but it was an attempt to make explicit the thing that the increment operator was to be applied to. One point which you should know is that the `*` and the increment/decrement operators all have the same precedence and they have right to left associativity (the reverse of most other operators in C). Perhaps this was not very obvious, but it is typical C code so here is a table showing you how to use the `*` and increment operators together.

Notation	Notation without ()	Meaning
++(*p)	++*p	Add 1 to the value of the object pointed to
(*p)++	(*p)++	Use the value of the object pointed to and then add 1 to it
*(p++)	*p++	Use the value of the object pointed to and then increment the pointer
*(++p)	*++p	Increment the pointer and then get the value of the object it now points to

Language-specific features

Arrays are converted to pointers in C

As was previously stated, the name of an array equates to the address of the first element (element 0) of that array. However, it should also be realized that each element of an array has an address and that through the use of pointers these addresses can be accessed directly. Furthermore, while the syntax of C allows you the use of indices for accessing arrays, what actually happens is that the index into the array is transformed by the compiler into a pointer, i.e. C does not use indices! How does this work?

Well, an expression such as `Number[4]` is replaced by the expression `*(Number + 4)`. Since `Number` is the name of an array it equates to an address, thus `Number + 4` becomes the address of the array element five up from the start. Thus `*(Number + 4)` returns the value held at that address. So why all this to-do about a somewhat arbitrary piece of conversion? The answer of course is efficiency. C is a language that is strongly focused on the hardware and pointers are another aspect of this same approach. A pointer (usually) actually holds the address of the thing it points to, whereas accessing an array through an index requires the address to be calculated.

In order to make use of this advantage, here is a piece of code which demonstrates array accessing through both indices and pointers. Each performs the same actions but the intention is for you to become familiar with using pointers.

```
#include <stdio.h>

main()
{
    int  Index;
    char CharArray[26];
    char *CharPtr;

    for (Index = 0; Index < 26; Index++)
    {
        CharArray[Index] = 'a' + Index;
    }

            /* CharPtr++ is an example of pointer */
            /* arithmetic and it is effectively   */
            /* current address + size of data type */

    for (CharPtr = CharArray; CharPtr < &CharArray[26]; CharPtr++)
    {
        printf("%c", *CharPtr);
    }
    printf("\n\nEnd of program.\n\n");
    return(0);
}
```

Examine the above program and convince yourself that the two `for` statements achieve the same array element access.

Initialization of pointers and arrays

You have seen that at compile time arrays can be initialized and further that arrays without dimensions can be sized during initialization. Take a look at the following:

```
char *words[]  =  {"hello", "you"};
```

Here `words` is an array of pointers to `char` and can be initialized with strings to create an array of pointers to strings, possibly each of different length. For this reason this is known as a ragged array, with uneven row length. It would be dangerous to attempt to access this array using row and column subscripts – so do not attempt it!

It is also possible to initialize a pointer to point to a character string literal, e.g.

```
char *ptr = "hello";
```

In this case the pointer points to an object of type array of `char` containing six elements (including the `null` terminator). However, beware; attempting to modify the contents of the array through `ptr` will result in undefined behaviour, so effectively the advice is not to attempt this.

If you were to define an array as:

```
char words[] = "hello";
```

then it would be fine to access the array using normal subscripts but remember there are six elements including the terminating null \0 character.

It is worth noting also that C does not provide any operators that act on whole strings, only on the character elements. To achieve things like concatenation of strings you must use the standard string handling libraries included with the header `<string.h>`.

See Appendix E dealing with the standard libraries and look up the string libraries in your manuals.

Command line arguments

The function `main()` can accept the command line from UNIX as its parameters. So if you create an executable program called `myprog` and run it as:

```
myprog take this line
```

then the components of this command line are available from inside the program. Look at the following simple example which merely prints out these command line components to the standard output (screen):

```
#include <stdio.h>

main(int argc, char *argv[])
```

```
{
      for (i=0; i<argc; i++)
            printf("%s ", argv[i]);
}
```

Using pointers, it could be written as:

```
#include <stdio.h>

main(int argc, char *argv[])
{
      while(*argv)
            printf("%s ", *argv++);
}
```

'argv' is a pointer to a `null` terminated array of pointers to null terminated strings.

The following diagram shows how argv points to the array of character strings in the example used:

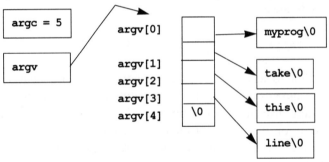

Summary for arrays and pointers

- Arrays are collections of data of the same type, e.g.

```
char   StockItems[NumOfItems][10]
int    ItemCount[NumOfItems - 1]
float  Price[NumOfItems - 1]
```

  Remember that an array name[5] contains elements name[0] to name[4].
- Arrays can be initialized, e.g.

```
char StockItems[NumOfItems][10] = {"Sugar", "Bread", "Salt",
                                    "Butter", "Milk", "Quit"};
int    ItemCount[NumOfItems - 1] = { 0,0,0,0,0};
float Price[NumOfItems - 1]   = {0.54, 0.76, 0.24, 0.59, 0.32};
```

If the dimensions are omitted then the compiler will compute the array size for one-dimensional arrays. For arrays of greater than one dimension only the first dimension can be omitted during initialization.

- Array parameters are passed by value, but, since the array name is actually the address of the first element, this is akin to pass by reference. Pass by reference is achieved by passing the address of a variable to a parameter of type pointer.

```
float GetCost(int *Quantity, float *Price);
TotalCost = GetCost(&Number, &Charge);
```

- Dereferencing is achieved using the dereferencing operator `*`, which can be treated as the 'contents of the address pointed to'.
  Arrays are converted to pointers in C. So `arrayname[4]` is really the same as `*(arrayname + 4)`.
- Pointer arithmetic is a powerful feature in C, particularly using the increment and decrement operators.

Notation	Notation without ()	Meaning
`++(*p)`	`++*p`	Add 1 to the value of the object pointed to.
`(*p)++`	`(*p)++`	Use the value of the object pointed to and then add 1 to it.
`*(p++)`	`*p++`	Use the value of the object pointed to and then increment the pointer.
`*(++p)`	`*++p`	Increment the pointer and then get the value of the nobject it now points to.

- Strings are `null` terminated arrays of characters.
- `main()` can accept the command line as parameter using:

```
main(int argc, char *argv[]);
```

where `argc` is the number of command line components including the program name and `argv` is a pointer to an array of pointers to the string components of the command line, e.g.

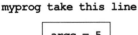

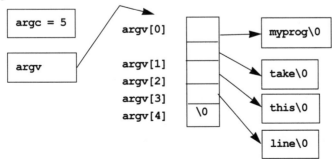

Exercises on arrays and pointers

4.5   Through the use of appropriate examples distinguish between the precedence and associativity of the following operators in C :

+ – *(i.e. multiplication operator) / ++ – *(i.e. operator dereference)

4.6   A software house has purchased a C compiler which does not have the library `string.h` and they need to create a set of generalized routines for validation and other useful activities. You are required to write the following three such routines:
(i) a function which will check that a given integer is in a given range and return 1 if this is true and 0 otherwise;
(ii) a function which will check that a given character is one of a set of characters passed as a string and return the index of the first occurence of that character in the string or –1 if the character is not in the string;
(iii) a function which will return the number of characters (excluding the `null` character) in a string.
In all cases the given numbers, characters, ranges and strings should be passed as parameters to the functions.

4.7   Using examples, explain the concept of pointer arithmetic in C.

Chapter 5

Data structures in C

OBJECTIVES

On completion of this chapter you will be able to:

☐ create and use data structures;

☐ use pointers to data structures;

☐ create and use variable-length data structures;

☐ create and use enumerated data types;

☐ create and use data type names which reflect the nature of problems.

The solution to many problems is centred on the capacity to structure the data present in those problems. Such structuring often involves grouping together logically related data and then devising routines which manipulate those groupings. Examples of this come from the realm of data processing which tackles problems concerning payroll, accounts, invoicing, stock control and so forth.

The aggregate data structures in C are the array, the `struct` and the `union`. Arrays you have met previously. This chapter introduces you to both `struct`s and `union`s. You will also meet enumerated data types, as supported by C, and a facility for associating names or identifiers with the base or user-defined data types. This latter capability is called `typedef`.

Records or `struct`s

As in other languages, the array in C allows you to create a grouping of objects of the same type and, while this is extremely useful for some sets of problems, it is quite inflexible where a problem solution involves the use of logically related data which is of different types, e.g. a person's name, age, gender etc. The `struct` gives you this extra level of flexibility because it lets you group together objects of the base data types, arrays and other `struct`s to form a single object.

The problem

Consider the following problem:

A corner shop is also a newspaper seller and it takes ten daily and twelve weekly titles. For each title the shop knows the name of the title, its publication frequency, the number received, the number ordered by customers, the number sold, the wholesale price, the retail price and the weekly profit.

Create appropriate data structures to represent this information. Use these data structures to write a C program which contains functions to read in the appropriate information for one title and also to determine which of the titles is the most profitable.

The program

float.h **contains a constant** FLT_MIN **which the program uses later.**

```
#include <stdio.h>
#include <float.h>
#define TitleLength 20
#define NumTitles 22

struct NewsRecord
{
        char Title[TitleLength];
        char PaperType;
        int NumReceived;
        int NumSold;
        float RetailPrice;
        float WholeSalePrice;
        float Profit;
```

Note the semi-colon after the closing }

```
};

main()
```

Function GetTitleDetails() **returns a** struct.

```
{
        struct NewsRecord GetTitleDetails(void);
        int MaxProfit(struct NewsRecord []);

        struct NewsRecord Papers[NumTitles];
        int Index;

                        /* start of main program */
        printf("\n\nGet the newspaper titles\n\n");
        for (Index = 0; Index < NumTitles; Index++)
        {
                Papers[Index] = GetTitleDetails();
        }
        printf("\n\nThe paper with the most profit is %-25s\n",
                Papers[MaxProfit(Papers)].Title);
```

```
        printf("\n\nProgram ends.\n\n");
        return(0);
}


struct NewsRecord GetTitleDetails(void)
{
        struct NewsRecord NewsPaper;
        float PriceDifference;

        printf("\nEnter Title, Publication PaperType, Number"
                " ordered, Number Sold, Retail Price"
                "Wholesale price\n ");
        scanf("%s %c %d %d %f %f",NewsPaper.Title,
                &NewsPaper.PaperType,
                &NewsPaper.NumReceived,
        &NewsPaper.NumSold,
                &NewsPaper.RetailPrice,
                &NewsPaper.WholeSalePrice);

        PriceDifference = NewsPaper.RetailPrice -
                                NewsPaper.WholeSalePrice;
        NewsPaper.Profit = (NewsPaper.NumSold *
                        PriceDifference) -
                        ((NewsPaper.NumReceived -
                        NewsPaper.NumSold) *
                        PriceDifference);
        return(NewsPaper);
}

int MaxProfit(struct NewsRecord Papers[])
{
        int MaxIndex;
        float ThisProfit = FLT_MIN;

        int Index = 0;

        for (MaxIndex = Index = 0; Index < NumTitles; Index++)
        {
                if (Papers[Index].Profit > ThisProfit)
                {
                        Profit = Papers[Index].ThisProfit;
                        MaxIndex = Index;
                }
        }
        return(MaxIndex);
}
```

Note the use of `scanf()` here with multiple arguments. You must ensure that the type of each input matches its input specifier or a runtime error may occur.

Return the initialized `struct` just as you would return any other value.

`FLT_MIN` is defined in `float`.h.

Multiple assignment is valid in C.

Let us now examine some of the issues arising from this example program.

Creating the `struct`

Here the obvious requirement is an array of records and this is obtained in C as follows:

```
struct NewsRecord
{
     char Title[25];
     char PaperType;
     int NumReceived;
     int NumOrdered;
     int NumSold;
     float WholesalePrice;
     float RetailPrice;
     float Profit;
} ;
struct NewsRecord Papers[NumTitles];
```

See the notes at the end of this chapter on creating `enums` in C.

In the above `struct` there is an assumption that the `PaperType` will be distinguished by using `w` for a weekly newspaper and `d` for a daily one. You can create enumerated data types in C though they are slightly different to those in languages such as Pascal or Modula-2.

Effectively the first declaration above creates a new type which you can then use to declare variables of that new type. Thus in the simple example above a `struct` is used to create a new type `struct NewsRecord` which contains fields comprising strings, `int`s and `float`s, and then `struct NewsRecord` is itself used to declare an array of 22 instances of `NewsRecord` structures, i.e. an array of `struct`s. In this sequence of events the name `NewsRecord` serves as a `Tagfield` for the name of the new type. In order to access a field of a `struct` variable you specify the `struct` variable name followed by a full stop and the field name, e.g.

```
strcpy(Papers[0].Title, "The Times");
Papers[0].RetailPrice = 0.25;
```

You can also assign the value of one `NewsRecord` variable to another, e.g.

```
Papers[19] = Papers[0];
```

Unions are discussed later in this Chapter.

Note, however, that assignment is the only operation on whole structures which C supports directly; there are no operators for comparison etc. This is due to the possible inclusion of `union`s within a `struct`. Another point to consider is that structures can require substantial amounts of memory and so when using them as arguments to functions it is common practice to pass a pointer to a struct rather than the actual struct itself. One further restriction which is applied to structs is that a struct cannot contain a recursive declaration, i.e.

```
struct InvalidDeclaration
{
        char Name[20];
        struct InvalidDeclaration BadField;
};
```

Functions can return structs

```
        struct NewsRecord GetTitleDetails(void)
        return(NewsPaper);
```

You have previously seen examples of functions which return values of type int, float and char. ANSI Standard C also allows you to return instances of user defined types from functions. Thus the function GetTitleDetails(void) returns to the function main() a struct which is then assigned to an element of the array Papers.

Functions can accept arrays of structs as parameters

```
        int MaxProfit(struct NewsRecord Papers[])
```

There is no difficulty in passing arrays of structs as parameters to functions; the syntax is just the same as with arrays of ints, floats etc. The description needed for the function prototype requires only the type, struct NewsRecord and the nature of the parameter, []. Thus this function prototype informs the compiler that the single argument for the function MaxProfit should be an array of structs of type NewsRecord. You should remember that in C when you pass an array as an argument you actually pass the address of that array, i.e. it is a pass-by-reference argument.

Pointers and structs

It should be obvious that structs and arrays of structs may need quite large amounts of memory and that passing them around as arguments to functions would be pretty costly in terms of memory. Just to reinforce the point made in the previous section, you cannot pass arrays of structs as call-by-value parameters to functions, but you can pass a single struct as a value parameter. This potential memory requirement is why it is common to pass pointers to structs as function parameters.

If the most sensible form of passing structs as parameters is through the use of pointers then you need to know how to create pointers to structures and also how to access the fields of structs through pointers. Declaring pointers is simple enough:

```
struct NewsRecords *PaperPtr;
struct NewsRecords Paper;
```

Here, the pointer *PaperPtr refers to nothing,

Title and
RetailPrice fields of
the *NewsRecord* object
pointed to by
PaperPtr.

and accessing the fields is done by using the operator ->, e.g.

```
PaperPtr = &Paper;      /* make PaperPtr point at a */
                        /* a NewsRecord struct.     */
strcpy(PaperPtr->Title,"The Times");
PaperPtr->RetailPrice = 0.25;
```

In the way that you can qualify the base data types you can also qualify these user defined types and thus you can specify that an object is const, volatile etc. In the same way you can qualify the data type of a parameter to a function as const, such that you explicitly prevent that function from modifying the value of that parameter, e.g.

```
void DisplayData(const struct NewsRecord);
```

Here the function DisplayData() is given a struct parameter of type NewsRecord but it is not allowed to modify the values of the fields of that parameter. This can be used to good effect to assist the future maintenance of code because you can explicitly show which functions are allowed to modify parameters.

In the same way, where you create a new data type and then declare a variable or pointer of such a type and qualify the declaration as const, then you cannot modify the value in that variable using assignment. For example, consider the following code:

```
main()
{
```

StudentPtr points to
first element of array
Results.

```
        struct StudentMark    /* create the new data type */
        {
                char Name[30];
                int Mark;
        };
```

ConstStructPtr also
points at the first
element of the array
Results, BUT is not
allowed to modify that
element.

```
        struct StudentMark Results[10], *StudentPtr;
        const struct StudentMark *ConstStructPtr;

        StudentPtr = Results;
        StudentPtr->Mark = 72;

        ConstStructPtr = Results;
        ConstStructPtr-> Mark += 5;  /* illegal operation */
}
```

The above example allows us to raise an issue which may not be apparent and that is the distinction between a const pointer and a pointer to a const struct. The `ConstStructPtr` in the above example is an example of a pointer to a `const struct` and the effect of such a declaration is to allow you to make `ConstStructPtr` point to any `struct` of type `StudentMark` but not to use it to change the fields of that `struct`.

The following declaration creates a `const` pointer to `structs` of type `StudentMark`:

```
struct StudentMark FirstMark;
struct StudentMark const *ConstPtr = &FirstMark;
```

The effect of this declaration is to to make `ConstPtr` point only at the struct `FirstMark`, i.e. you cannot make it point at other `structs` of type `StudentMark`. You can how ever use `ConstPtr` to change the value of any of the fields in `StudentMark`. This also has implications when declaring `const` parameters, and the same rules apply.

Initializing structs at the point of declaration
As with arrays, you can give `struct` fields values when you declare them and the mechanism is very like that for arrays. A simple example might be the creation of a catalogue of books which held the Title, Author, ISBN number and cost of each book:

```
struct Book
{
        char *Title;
        char *Author;
        long int ISBN;
        float Cost;
}

struct Book Catalogue[MaxBooks] = { {"Pride and Prejudice",
                          "Jane Austen", 032118976,
                        26.50},
                        {"Bleak House", "Charles
                        Dickens",
                          032118852, 31.99},
                        {"Jude the Obscure", "Thomas
                        Hardy",
                          032118810, 22.95}
                        };
```

Note that in element 0 the ISBN field is uninitialized, and that element 1 is completely uninitialized.

Notice that in initializing the elements of the array `Catalogue` the values for the field of each element are contained within a pair of `{}`, and the whole initialization is itself enclosed in outer pair of `{}`. Remember that the order of the initialization values is important and must match the type of the relevant field. Again strings are enclosed in double quotes and commas separate both the field values and the element initializers. Where there is no initial value for a field or element, then its absence should be indicated by two consecutive commas, e.g.

```
struct Book Catalogue[MaxBooks] = {
                    {"Pride and Prejudice", "Jane Austen",,
                     26.50},
                    /* no initialiser for element 1 */ ,
                    {"Jude the Obscure", "Thomas Hardy",
                     032118810, 22.95}
                                };
```

Exercises on data structures

5.1   Devise a `struct` date which represents the date as follows:
– an integer for the day;
– a string for the month;
– an integer for the year.

5.2   Devise a `struct` for the personnel records of a company which stores the following information about each of its staff:
– name;
– date of birth;
– salary;
– NHS number;
– position;
– date of joining the company.
Make use of the date `struct` you defined in Exercise 5.1 to assist you here.

5.3   (i) Outline the characteristics which distinguish the array from the struct in the C programming language. Give an example of a situation where you would choose to use each data structure in preference to the other.
(ii) A Local Education Authority (LEA) has 59 schools, each of which belongs to one of the following categories; infant, junior, secondary, sixth form or college. Each school has a name, an address and a unique reference number. Fire safety regulations stipulate that the number and location (the floor and room number) of every fire exit in a school must be known. Equally the number of staff and pupils in each school must also be known. For each member of staff their grade (Head, Senior Teacher, Junior Teacher, Infants Teacher, Admin. Staff), name and salary are known. For pupils their name, age, desk number and mobility (able bodied, wheel-chair bound, assisted walker) are

also known. A school can employ a maximum of 50 staff and no
school can have more than 500 pupils.

At present this information is held on sets of cards. The LEA is considering computerizing this information and you are required to create
suitable data structures to represent the information. Having done so,
declare an appropriate data structure for the 59 schools in this LEA.

(iii) Write a C function which accepts as an argument an instance of
the data structure devised in part (ii) and which returns the number of
wheel-chair-bound pupils for the specified school.

Unions (similar to variant records)

The difference between a `struct` and a `union` is that in the former each field
is allocated its own storage, and therefore its own type, and that memory is
consecutive, whereas in a `union` each field is allocated the same piece of
memory and it is up to you, the programmer, to decide which field is to be
represented. It should be apparent that the actual amount of memory allocated to a `union` will be that which is large enough to hold a value of the type
requiring the most memory; all other possible types can be represented
within that memory.

What purpose does a `union` serve? Going back to C's emphasis on efficiency of execution and storage, `union`s allow you to identify cases where a
variable can assume one of several mutually exclusive possible types and
thus save memory by only ever using that for the largest type. Another use
is within a struct where there are several distinct but very similar groupings.
Here a `union` can be used such that a single `struct` can be declared and a
`union` used to describe the difference between the groupings. This is the
most sensible way of using `union`s because you can include within the
`struct` a field which contains a value indicating which of the possible forms
of the variant is being used at any time.

Here is a simple program to illustrate the use of unions in C. The program
creates a `struct` which contains a `union` whose alternatives include an `int`,
a `float` and a `char`. A `Tagfield` `Unionfield` is used to indicate the type of value
currently held in the `union`. Thus the code initializes the `union` in several
different ways and prints out the results correctly.

```
#include <stdio.h>
#define NameLength 20

struct VariantRecord
{
        char Name[NameLength];
        int Unionfield;
        union
```

`Unionfield` uses 0 to indicate that union is a `char`, 1 for an `int`, and 2 for a `float`.

```
                    {
                            char CharVal;
                            int  IntVal;
                            float FloatVal;
                    } VarField;
          };
```

VarField **is the identifier for this** union.

```
int main()
{
        void GetDetails(struct VariantRecord *Record);
        void PrintDetails(const struct VariantRecord *Record);

        struct VariantRecord Example;

        printf("\n\n Get the Details for the "
                                        "Variant Record\n\n");
        GetDetails(&Example);
        PrintDetails(&Example);

        printf("\n\nChange the variant part.\n\n");
        Example.UnionField = 1;
        Example.VarField.IntVal = 4096;
        PrintDetails(&Example);

        Example.UnionField = 2;
        Example.VarField.FloatVal = 123456.789;
        PrintDetails(&Example);

        printf("\n\nProgram finishes here.\n\n");
        return(0);
}

void GetDetails(struct VariantRecord *Record)
{
        printf("\n\nEnter the name ..> ");
        scanf("%s", Record->Name);
        Record->UnionField = 0;
        Record->VarField.CharVal = '*';
}
```

Note the use of the const **qualifier here for the argument** *Record. **If a local pointer is assigned the same value as** *Record **then it must also be** const **qualified.**

```
void PrintDetails(const struct VariantRecord *Record)
{

        printf("\nName =%20s UnionField =%2d Value = ",
                Record->Name, Record->UnionField);
```

```
        switch (Record->UnionField)
        {
                case 0 : {printf(" %2c\n\n",
                                Record->VarField.CharVal);
                         break;
                         }
                case 1 : {printf("%8d\n\n",
                                Record->VarField.IntVal);
                         break;
                         }
                case 2 : {printf("%10.2f\n\n",
                                Record->VarField.FloatVal);
                         break;
                         }

        }
}
```

Let us examine some of the issues arising from this program.

Accessing the union field in the struct VariantRecord

```
        Example.VarField.IntVal = 4096;
        Record->VarField.FloatVal;
```

The two statements in the box above show you how to access the union field called `VarField` within the `struct VariantRecord`. The first statement is taken from the function `main()` where `Example` is a variable of type `struct VariantRecord` and the union field is accessed in just the same way as you would access a field in a `struct` nested within a `struct`. The second statement is taken from the function `PrintDetails`, where `RecPtr` is a pointer to an instance of type `struct VariantRecord`. Here the accessing is done as a pointer to the union field and then as a `struct` to the specific field within the union. The following diagram gives you another view on this aspect of accessing fields within `struct`s:

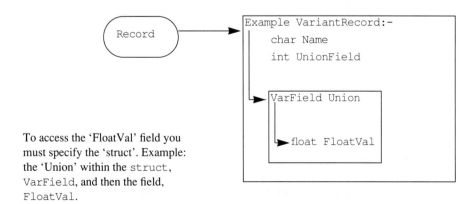

To access the 'FloatVal' field you must specify the 'struct'. Example: the 'Union' within the struct, VarField, and then the field, FloatVal.

Setting the Tagfield before assigning a value to the union field.

> **Example.Unionfield = 2;**
>
> **Example.VarField.FloatVal = 123456.789;**

Notice how the Unionfield is set before assigning the real value to the union field. You should pay particular attention to the fact that the value assigned to the Tagfield based on a convention that you, the programmer, must decide on and adhere to. In this case the program assumed a convention of 0 for a character, 1 for an integer and 2 for a real number. Having chosen this convention, the program then uses it consistently. Thus setting Unionfield to 2 means that the union field to be accessed is the real number one. You can of course ignore this and place a value into the union as an integer and use it as a float, BUT this is both extremely bad programming practice and also is highly likely to produce unpredictable results!

Enumerations in C

Those of you who have met enumerated data types in Pascal or Modula-2 may find the enum facility in C a little different. It allows you to create a data type in which you can specify the values that a variable of that type can assume. As an example consider the following enum declaration:

```
enum Colours
{
        Red, White, Blue, Yellow, Green, Indigo
};
```

Here the individual entries in the enum have values 0, 1, 2, 3, 4, 5 and 6 respectively. Remember that anything C does with regard to bounds is to assign 0 as the lower bound hence Red has value 0 and not 1. Thus a variable declared of type Colours can assume values of Red, White, Blue etc. which is in effect 0, 1, 2 and so on. This is really a diminished form of enumerated data type in comparison to that in Pascal and Modula-2.

C does allow you to control the allocation of values to the entries in an enum type by specifying which value an entry is to be associated with, e.g.

```
enum FileStatus
{
        Fail, Success, DoesNotExist = 3, IncorrectMode,
        NotAllowedAccess
};
```

Once a value has been forced onto an entry, the subsequent entries continue their numbering sequence from that value, i.e. here IncorrectMode would have the value 4 associated with it, NotAllowedAccess would take the value 5.

The major advance provided by enums is that without them you would need to create symbolic constants using #defines. enums provide more control over the scope of their declaration because they fall within the usual scope rules for C whereas #define has a scope defined by its position within the source file. enums do greatly improve readability.

typedef – creating type names which reflect the nature of a problem

The typedef facility provides you, the programmer, with a mechanism for associating a particular identifier with a given type. One use of this is to create identifiers which relate to the elements of a specific problem solution and to use them rather than the usual C types when declaring and defining variables, specifying function prototypes and so forth. A simple example of this could be a problem where the suits of a pack of playing cards need to be represented, thus:

```
typedef int CardSuits;
CardSuits Hearts, Spades, Clubs, Diamonds;
```

Here CardSuits is used instead of int for declaring the different suits, though Hearts, Spades etc. are actually ints. A more interesting example might be where a problem contains a description of the characteristics of a car and then needs to refer to instances, e.g. of a Ford car, or a Vauxhall car. This might look something like the following:

```
struct car
{
        char *model;
        int NumOfWheels;
        int NumOfPassengers;
        int EngineCapacity;
};
typedef struct car car;
car Ford, Vauxhall;
```

In this example the typedef is used to associate the Tagfield for the struct with itself, i.e. a variable of type car is in reality a variable of type struct car. It can be argued that this use of typedef improves the readability of C programs incorporating helpful names. While this is perhaps contentious, it can be seen that creating typedefs for multidimensional arrays of structs which are passed as arguments to functions does lead to simpler function interfaces.

Language-specific features

Bitfields and `structs`

C provides a mechanism for creating small elements of data as the fields of a `struct`. Here the fields may be described as a number of bits rather than the base data types. The most obvious uses of such things is in minimizing data storage or specifically to get at some of the bits of fields of `structs`, particularly when accessing data in files produced by other applications.

Bitfields are of little use for most non-systems programming problems and so you are referred to both the ANSI Standard C reference manual and the manual for your C compiler for further details.

`structs` and the ANSI Standard

With respect to the ANSI standard there are several points to bear in mind when using `structs`:

- memory for fields in a `struct` is allocated in the order in which they appear in the `struct` declaration;
- nothing will be inserted before the first field of a `struct` (because of memory boundary alignment, it is common for compilers to insert blank bytes within structures to ensure the easy storage and retrieval of stored data);
- the address of the first field of a struct can also be taken as the address for the whole `struct` if the appropriate cast operator is applied;
- bit fields have no addresses but they are grouped into units and are subject to the three points above. There are no pointers to, nor arrays of, bitfields.

Summary for data structures

- Generalized forms for defining and declaring a `struct` are:

```
struct Tagfield                      struct Tagfield
    {                                    {
        type1 field1;                        type1 field1;
        type2 field2;        OR              type2 field2;
            .                                    .
        typeN fieldN;                        typeN fieldN;
    };                               }  VariableName;

struct Tagfield VariableName;
```

- The general form of defining and declaring `enum` data types is:

```
enum Tagfield
{enumeration1, enumeration2, . . .enumerationN
```

```
};
```

enum Tagfield EnumVariable;

- Typedefs are defined and declared as:

```
typedef CurrentTypeDefinition NewIdentifier;
```

Exercises on data structures, enumerations and typedefs

5.4   The organizers of a forthcoming art exhibition wish to record the title, artist, type (i.e. painting, sculpture, ceramic or craft work), artist's address and price of each exhibit with a view to producing a catalogue for the public. Create suitable data structures to represent this information and then write a C program which prompts a user for the relevant information and stores that in an array of the resultant data structure. Incorporate suitable code to print the catalogue of exhibits.

5.5   A second-hand car dealer wants to create a simple database which contains the manufacturer, model, price, age, mileage, colour and engine size of all the cars in stock. Once this has been done, routines are needed to retrieve cars by manufacturer and price range. On such retrievals zero, one or more cars may be found. Create an appropriate data structure, CarDetails, to represent the information for this database, and then declare an array of 10 such structs. Write a C program containing a function which prompts the dealer for the details of one car and **returns** a struct containing these details. Use this function to initialize the elements of the array of the CarDetails for this dealer. Write a second function which will prompt a user for the the manufacturer of a car and the price range they can afford. Write a function which will search your CarDetails array and print out all cars which are built by the specified manufacturer and fall within the given price range.

5.6   A library wishes to computerize its lending system and, as an aid to this, it has been decided that the following information is needed on each borrower: name and address, the number of books they have on loan; whether they have any books overdue; and the amount of outstanding fines they owe the library.
With regard to the books a borrower has on loan the library needs to know the title, author, book number, book classification and the date that it is due for return. The date is held in the form day, month and year, each of which is held as a whole number. No user may have more than ten books on loan at any one time. The library classifies its books as reference, non-fiction, adventure, thriller and sci-fi.
Create appropriate data structures to represent this information and

then use them in a C program which allows users to borrow and return books, and also checks to see if a user has any books which are overdue. Where a book is overdue a fine is levied at a rate of 20 pence per book per week or part thereof and the relevant information for that borrower should be updated accordingly.

It is suggested that you initialize some arrays with the details of some borrowers and books, i.e. don't write functions to enter, modify, insert or delete borrowers or books unless you wish to make this a major piece of work. In order to simplify the calculation for the dates, use 1990 as the base year and calculate the number of days which have elapsed since 1 January of that year.

Chapter 6

Dynamic data structures

OBJECTIVES

On completion of this chapter you will be able to:

☐ create and use data structures while your programs are running;

☐ release the memory allocated to dynamically created data structures;

☐ process data held as a linked list;

☐ deal with some common errors which arise from linked list processing.

You have already met data structures which are defined either statically or automatically. Structures defined in this fashion are allocated a fixed amount of memory at compile time regardless of the actual amount of memory that will be used or needed. This memory is allocated for the life-time of the block in which those data structures are defined. It should be clear that for extreme cases there might be a possibility of such data structures being too small to contain the data. This leads to programmers attempting to determine the maximum possible amount of memory required and always allocating this. Such an approach is often extremely wasteful of the memory resource.

Another problem associated with statically defining arrays arises with the need either to insert a new or to delete an existing element of the array. It is usual to manipulate array elements physically in order to accommodate this action. This processing can have very high overheads when the arrays are large.

The full power of C is evident in the use of dynamically allocated memory for data structures, as this combines pointers and data structures to obtain memory of just the right size for exactly the length of time it is needed. This memory allocation occurs at run time and is effected through calls to functions available as a result of the inclusion of the header file `<stdlib.h>`.

Dynamic data structures allow programmers to request specific amounts of memory at run time. In this way only that memory immediately required is allocated. There is also the ability to free such memory as and when the need for it disappears. Thus, for situations where the amount of data being processed is unknown, one can use dynamic data structures to grab more memory as and when it is needed. This gives the programmer much greater control over memory resources.

Equally, structures where arrays are used can be dealt with dynamically by determining the actual dimension of these arrays at run time. Another typical application might be where the data can be held as a series of linked lists. For a simple example consider the data structures needed for a primitive editor dealing with pages of text. Here there would be a linked list of pages, each of which would comprise a linked list of lines of text. Each line would be composed of linked lists of words and each word would in turn comprise linked lists of characters. Dynamically allocated memory in such an application would ensure that only the memory necessary to hold the text for any one page was allocated.

A simple problem concerning cash machine transactions

A bank cash point provides customers who have valid account numbers with the facility to withdraw money, deposit money, obtain the value of the current balance and obtain a statement of any transactions which have been carried out. Each time a withdrawal or deposit is performed a copy of the nature of that transaction, the amount of cash involved and the old and new cash balances is created and added onto a list of other such transactions for that customer. When a statement of all the transactions is requested, any transactions recorded are printed and removed from the list so that at the end of this action the list of transactions for that customer becomes empty.

A solution

A bank allows customers to open accounts and for each account the bank holds the following information: the customer's name, address and current balance, as well the details of each transaction relating to the account. No one can predict the exact number of transactions which will occur for an account over a varying time period. This is an obvious use for dynamic memory allocation, whereby memory is requested as each transaction occurs. In this way only sufficient memory to hold the transactions which have occurred to date is used.

Structures of such accounts might look as follows:

```
Struct Customer
{
        char *Name;
        int AccountNo;
        float Balance;
        struct TransAction * TransList;
```

```
};

Struct TransAction
{
        struct Time Date;;
        char *Action;
        float Amount;
        float OldBalance;
        float NewBalance;
        struct TransAction  * Next;
};
```

Here the pointer `TransPtr` is used to indicate the start of the list of recorded transactions. Each time a transaction occurs, a piece of memory big enough to hold an instance of the `struct TransAction` is requested, its fields set and then it is linked on to the end of the list pointed to by the `TransPtr`.

Pseudocode solution
Loop continuously doing
    If there are no more customers
        close the cash point
    Else
        get the next customer
        If not a valid customer
            output a message to that effect
        Else
            While we are dealing with this customer
                display the menu of possible actions
                get the customer's choice
                If the choice is withdraw money
                    do withdraw cash action
                Elsif the choice is deposit money
                    do the deposit cash action
                Elsif the choice is display current balance
                    do print current balance action
                Elsif the choice is show the list of transactions
                    do print transaction list action
                Elsif the choice is quit
                    terminate this loop
                Else
                    output a message for the invalid choice
                End
            End While
        End
    End
End Loop

The program

```c
#include <stdio.h>
#include <stdlib.h>
#include <math.h>

#define LENGTH 20
/*#define DEBUG 1*/
#define CUSTOMERS 5

enum Transactions {WithDrawal = 1, Deposit, CurrentBalance,
        PrintStatement, Quit};

struct Time
{
    int Day;
    int Month;
    int Year;
};

struct Transaction
{
    struct Time Date;
    char *Action;        /* pointer to a string */
    float Amount;
    float OldBalance;
    float NewBalance;
    struct Transaction *Next;/* link to next transaction */
};

struct Customer
{
    char *Name;
    int AccountNo;
    float Balance;
    struct Transaction *TransList; /* head of transaction
                                          list */
};

void ReadLn(void)
{
    while ((getchar()) != '\n')
            ;
}

main()
```

```
{
            /* FUNCTION PROTOTYPES  */
    int NextCustomer(void);
    struct Customer * FindCustomer(struct Customer []);
    void ShowMenu(void);
    enum Transactions GetTransaction(void);
    void WithDrawCash(struct Customer *);
    void DepositCash(struct Customer *);
    void CashBalance(struct Customer *);
    void Statement(struct Customer *);

    struct Customer *CustomerPtr;
    enum Transactions Request;
    struct Customer Customers[CUSTOMERS] =
                { {"Peter Smith", 6678, 998.03, NULL},
                  {"Alice Jay", 7785, 1203.54, NULL},
                  {"Geoff Lane", 7786, 1104.01, NULL},
                  {"Jane Grey", 7787, 1206.99, NULL},
                  {"Lisa Mac", 6677, 778.12, NULL}
                };
    while(1)
    {
        if ((NextCustomer()) == -1)
        {
            printf("\nNo more customers, Cash Point closing\n");
            break;
        }
        else
        {
            if ((CustomerPtr = FindCustomer(Customers))
                                                    == NULL)
            {
                printf("\n\nNo such customer, start again!!");
            }
            else
            {
                do
                {
                  ShowMenu();
                  switch (Request = GetTransaction())
                  {
                    case WithDrawal    :{
                                        WithDrawCash(CustomerPtr);
                                        break;
                                        }
```

```
                        case Deposit        :{
                                    DepositCash(CustomerPtr);
                                    break;
                                        }
                    case CurrentBalance :{
                                    CashBalance(CustomerPtr);
                                    break;
                                        }
                    case PrintStatement :{
                                        Statement(CustomerPtr);
                                    break;
                                        }
                    case Quit           :{
                                    break;
                                        }
                    default             :{
                            printf("\n\nNo such transaction\n\n");
                                    break;
                                        }
                }       /* end of switch */
            } while (Request != Quit);/* end of do.while */
        }/* end the inner else */
    }/* end the outer else */
    }/* end the while infinite loop */
    exit(0);
}


int NextCustomer(void)
{
    int Reply;

    printf("\n\n\tAny More Customers?  ..> ");
    Reply = getchar();
    ReadLn();
    return(  (Reply == 'y') || (Reply == 'Y') ? 0 : -1);
}


struct Customer *FindCustomer(struct Customer Customers[])
    /***********************************************************/
    /* Returns a pointer to the actual element if a customer   */
    /* is found and the NULL pointer otherwise                 */
    /***********************************************************/
{
    struct Customer *CustPtr;
    int AccNo;
```

```c
#ifdef DEBUG
    printf("\n\nIn FindCustomer :");
#endif
    CustPtr = Customers;
    printf("\nEnter your account number [999] ..> ");
    scanf("%d", &AccNo);
    ReadLn();
    while ((CustPtr->AccountNo != AccNo) && (CustPtr <
&Customers[CUSTOMERS]))
    {
#ifdef DEBUG
    printf("\nSearching : AccNo =%d Name = %s", CustPtr->AccountNo,
                    CustPtr->Name);
#endif
        CustPtr++;
    }
    if (CustPtr->AccountNo != AccNo)
    {
        CustPtr = NULL;
    }
    return(CustPtr);
}


void ShowMenu(void)
{
    printf("\n\n\n\n\tSelect Option Required\n");
    printf("\t_____\n\n");
    printf("1)  Withdraw Cash\n\n");
    printf("2)  Deposit Cash\n\n");
    printf("3)  Print Current Balance\n\n");
    printf("4)  Print Account statement\n\n");
    printf("5)  Quit with no action\n\n");
    printf("Enter [1, 2, 3, 4, 5] ..> ");
}


enum Transactions GetTransaction(void)
{
    enum Transactions Value;

    scanf("%d", &Value);
    ReadLn();
    return(Value);
}


void AddTransaction(struct Customer *CustPtr, char *Name, float Value)
```

```c
/****************************************************************/
/* add a transaction to the transaction list for this customer.*/
/* Transactions added at the tail of the existing list         */
/****************************************************************/
{
    struct Transaction *TempPtr, *SearchPtr;
                        /* grab some memory for this transaction */
    if (TempPtr = malloc(sizeof(struct Transaction)))
    {
        TempPtr->Action = Name;
        TempPtr->Amount = Value;   /* value is -ve for a withdrawal
                                      and +ve for a deposit */
        TempPtr->NewBalance = CustPtr->Balance;
        TempPtr->OldBalance = CustPtr->Balance - Value;
        TempPtr->Next = NULL;

        SearchPtr = CustPtr->TransList;/*work pointer set to start
                                         of transactions */
        if (SearchPtr)          /* there are transactions already */
        {
            while (SearchPtr->Next)
            {
                SearchPtr = SearchPtr->Next;
            }
            SearchPtr->Next = TempPtr;
        }
        else /*start a new list, this is the first transaction*/
        {
            CustPtr->TransList = TempPtr;
        }
#ifdef DEBUG
    printf("\n\nCustomer Name = %20s Account No = %d"
                    ,CustPtr->Name,
                    CustPtr->AccountNo);
    TempPtr = CustPtr->TransList;
    while (TempPtr)
    {
        printf("\nAction = %s Value = %6.2f", TempPtr->Action,
                            TempPtr->Amount);
        TempPtr = TempPtr->Next;
    }
#endif
    }
}
void WithDrawCash(struct Customer *CustPtr)
```

```
{
    float Cash;

    printf("\n\nEnter the amount of cash you wish to withdraw.> ");
    scanf("%f", &Cash);
    ReadLn();
    if (Cash > CustPtr->Balance)
    {
        printf("\n\nWithdrawal prohibited: ");
        printf("too little cash in your account\n\n");
    }
    else
    {
        CustPtr->Balance -= Cash;
        AddTransaction(CustPtr, "Withdrawal", - Cash);
    }
}


void DepositCash(struct Customer *CustPtr)
{
    float Cash;

    printf("\n\nEnter the amount of cash you wish to deposit.> ");
    scanf("%f", &Cash);
    ReadLn();
    CustPtr->Balance += Cash;
    AddTransaction(CustPtr, "Deposit", Cash);
}


void CashBalance(struct Customer *CustPtr)
{
    printf("\n\nYour current cash balance is %8.2f\n\n",
                                    CustPtr->Balance);
}


void Statement(struct Customer *CustPtr)

/***********************************************************/
/* print the existing list of transactions and release the  */
/* memory allocated for them.                              */
/***********************************************************/
{
    struct Transaction *TransPtr, *TempPtr;

    printf("\n\n\tCustomer Name = %-20s Account No = %4d"
```

```
                                    , CustPtr->Name,CustPtr->AccountNo);
    printf("\n\n\tTransaction\tAmount\tOld Balance\tNew Balance");
    printf("\n\n\t_____");
    printf("_____");
    if (! CustPtr->TransList)
    {
        printf("\n\n\t\tNo Transactions recorded for this
Customer\n\n");
    }
    else
    {
        TransPtr = CustPtr->TransList;
        CustPtr->TransList = NULL;    /* reset the head of the
                                        transactions list */
        while (TransPtr)
        {
            printf("\n\t%11s%10.2f%12.2f%15.2f",TransPtr->Action,
                fabs(TransPtr->Amount), TransPtr->OldBalance,
                                        TransPtr->NewBalance);
            TempPtr = TransPtr;
            TransPtr = TransPtr-> Next;
            free(TempPtr);
        }
    }
}
```

Let's discuss some interesting aspects of this program.

Pointers as fields in structs

```
                struct Transaction * Next
                struct Transaction *TransList
```

Here the pointers are declared as fields in the struct definitions and are used to link together instances of the same data type. In the struct Transaction there is a recursive inclusion since the field Next is itself a pointer to data of type Transaction. This allows a linked list of elements of this data type to be constructed dynamically. In the struct called Customer the field TransList is also of type Transaction and is used to act as the start of the list of transactions for a customer. If this pointer is null then no transactions have occurred, and, if it is not null, then it points to the struct which details the first transaction.

Initialization of pointer fields in structs

```
                struct Customer Customers[CUSTOMERS] =
                        { {"Peter Smith", 6678, 998.03, NULL}
```

.

```
        .
    }
```

This example shows once again the initialization of array elements at the point of definition. Here there is an array of `Customer` structs and one field of such a `struct` is a pointer to an instance of a `Transaction` struct. In order to give this field a known value the only sensible thing to do is to make it a `null` pointer and that is what is done above. The first three values, a string, an `int` and a `float` are assigned to the `Name`, `AccountNo` and `Balance` fields while the `null` value is assigned to the `TransList` field.

Infinite loops

```
                    while(1)
```

This is an example of an infinite loop. The processing, once started, will only terminate in exceptional circumstances. If you check the code within this loop you will see that there is a specific test which is used to stop the loop and this could have been extracted and used to control this loop. We chose not to do so since the nature of the example is such that the cash dispenser would remain operating for successive customers until it ran out of cash or some mechanical fault occurred. We do not, in this example, check the stock of cash which could have been implemented.

Passing undimensioned arrays as arguments to functions

```
        struct Customer *Find Customer(struct Customer Customers[])
```

Notice that the argument to this function is an array of `Customer`, but that no dimension is given to the formal parameter `Customers`. Essentially this is rather like saying that what is expected is a pointer to elements of an array of unknown size. The size could be unknown because it is determined at run time or it could be that only a part of an array is to be passed, i.e. the address of an element beyond the first element is given.

Dynamically allocating memory

```
if (TempPtr = malloc(sizeof (struct Transaction)))
{
        TempPtr->Action = Name;

        .

        .

        TempPtr->Next = NULL;
}
```

This call explicitly requests memory at run time to hold the details of some new transaction. The test is there to ensure that the call is successful and that the pointer returned does point at an area of memory big enough to hold an instance of a `Transaction` struct. Once the memory has been obtained, then the fields are initialized with the details for the transaction. The pointer field is set to `null`.

'Walking' down linked lists

```
SearchPtr = CustPtr->TransList;
if (SearchPtr)
{
        while (SearchPtr->Next)
        {
                SearchPtr = SearchPtr->Next;
        }
        SearchPtr->Next = TempPtr;
}
else
{
        CustPtr->TransList = TempPtr;
}
```

An arbitrary decision was taken that, in this example, each new transaction would be added to the end of the existing list of transactions for any given customer. Hence, having created a new instance of a `Transaction` we need to find the end of the list of transactions for the current customer. To do that we must start at the head of that customer's transaction list, the field `TransList`, and traverse each transaction until we find the last one. For this we use a temporary work pointer, `SearchPtr`, which we set to point to the same thing as the pointer of the head of that customer's transaction list and check to see first if the work pointer is the `null` pointer, in which case there are no transactions for this customer so far. Thus we make that customer's `TransList` point to this new transaction. Otherwise we check the `Next` field for each transaction; if it is not the `null` pointer, then there is at least one more transaction on the list and so we set the work pointer `SearchPtr` to point to this next transaction and check the `Next` field of that. This continues until the `Next` field is `null` at which point we have reached the end of the transaction list and so we can add our new transaction here. This is achieved by making the `Next` pointer of the transaction, pointed to by the work pointer `SearchPtr`, point to the new transaction.

Releasing dynamically allocated memory at runtime

```
TransPtr = CustPtr->TransList;
        while (TransPtr)
        {
                printf("\n\t%11s%10.2f%12.2f%15.2f",
                        TransPtr->Action, TransPtr->Amount,
                        TransPtr->OldBalance, TransPtr->NewBalance);
                TempPtr = TransPtr;
```

```
        TransPtr = TransPtr->Next;
        free(TempPtr);
    }
```

This segment of code illustrates that part of the process which prints out the contents of the transaction list for the current customer. Once again it involves walking down the linked list of transactions, starting at the head. This time the details held for each transaction are printed out and the memory used to hold those details is released for use by the rest of the program. Notice here that a second work pointer `TempPtr` is set to point to the transaction element whose details have just been printed, the first work pointer, `TransPtr`, is set to point to the next transaction and then the function `free()` is called. This sequence is important. If you were to call `free()` and give it `TransPtr` as the argument it would certainly release the memory pointed to by `TransPtr` but this would also lose our pointer into the list of transactions.

Common errors in linked list processing

Programmers who are unfamiliar with linked list programming often have difficulty in several areas. This section indicates some of these problems and the nature of such confusion.

Pointers are bound by types

When a programmer declares a pointer, the syntax of such a declaration explicitly states that such a pointer can only point to variables of the given type, e.g.

```
int *IntPtr;
```

Here `IntPtr` declares a pointer variable of type `int`. As such it cannot be made to point to variables of type `float`. A typical error of naive programmers is to assume that a pointer value can point to anything. This is patently not the case although through the use of casting and the `void` type this can be achieved.

The programmer frequently confuses the address held in the pointer with the contents of the address pointed to by the pointer

Where a programmer intends to add a value to the contents of the memory pointed to by a pointer, they actually add that value to the contents of the pointer. This can have unusual results, e.g.

```
int   * IntPtr;
int     IntValue = 12;
```

```
IntPtr  =    & IntValue;
IntPtr += 1;
```

Here `IntPtr` is assigned the address of the variable `IntValue`. Adding one to `IntPtr` actually increments the address it holds, i.e. It no longer points at `IntValue`. To add one to the variable `IntValue` through the use of pointer `IntPtr`. requires the application of the dereference operator, i.e.

```
*IntPtr  +=  1;
```

Undefined pointers
Declaring a pointer only gets a piece of memory large enough to hold an address. The content of such memory is not initialized and is thus indeterminate. Referencing such pointers often has undesirable side effects, the usual results being `Bus Error` or `segmentation violation`. Please note that a `null` pointer is not undefined.

`null` pointers
The following pointer is one such that it is explicitly set to point to nothing. Accessing such a pointer is valid, it is typically the last pointer in a list. However, programmers should remember that, since a `null` pointer points at nothing, no attempt should be made to reference the fields of the data structure to which that pointer could point.

Processing beyond the end of lists
A common programming error is to walk down a list to the last element and then to attempt to move beyond that point. This is often due to an incorrect algorithm.

Linking new nodes into existing lists
When linking a new node into an existing list, a new node must be made to point to the relevant node in the list and the preceding node must be made to point to the new node. The sequence in which this linking occurs is important. Programmers should remember to make the new node point into the list before making the list point to the new node.

Language-specific features

Memory allocation for multiple items
Where there is a requirement for obtaining memory for several instances of a data structure at run time, then rather than use several calls to `malloc()` an alternative function `calloc()` can be used. The format of such calls is:

```
void *calloc(size_t, size_t);
```

Here is a simple example to illustrate this:

```
float *TablePtr, Object;
TablePtr = calloc(10, sizeof(Object));
```

Here the first argument indicates the number of instances of an `object` for which memory is required, and the second gives the amount of memory needed to store one instance of the `object`. This mechanism is particularly useful for creating dynamic arrays in C. As with `malloc()`, this function returns a pointer of type `void` to the area of memory big enough to hold the `number` instances of type `object`. Where the call fails then a `null` pointer is returned. A successful call also means that the memory allocated will be initialized to zero. Again `calloc()` is typically associated with the use of the `sizeof` operator. Here is a further example:

```
int *ColumnPtr, Number = 25;
ColumnPtr = calloc(Number, sizeof(int));
```

Here `ColumnPtr` is fixed to point to a linear (one-dimensional) array of integers in which there are 20 elements.

With regard to choosing between the use of `malloc()` or `calloc()` here is a rule of thumb:

if you are allocating arrays
       use `calloc()`
else if you need the allocated memory to be initialized to a known value
       use `calloc()`
else
       use `malloc()` .

Casting the pointer returned by a call to `malloc()` or `calloc()`.
The mechanism through which various languages achieve dynamic memory allocation tends to be specific to each language. There is one particular feature of the C mechanism which is quite specific to it, namely the ability to assign the pointer returned by the call to pointer variables of any type.

Looking at the prototype for either of the dynamic memory allocation functions, you should notice that the type of the pointer returned is `void`. This allows that pointer to be assigned to pointer variables of any type and is an extension of the mechanism which existed in the earlier versions of C. Here the calls returned a pointer to an `int` and these had to be explicitly cast to allow assignment to pointer variables for other types, e.g.:

```
RecordPtr =  (RecordPtr*) malloc(sizeof(Record));
```

ANSI compatible C compilers will allow this form of the call and from a maintenance viewpoint explicitly casting the pointer gives a clear statement to any reader of the code that such a manipulation is indeed what is intended.

Summary for dynamic data structures

Memory allocation for single items
Dynamic memory allocation is achieved through calling the function `malloc()` which is accessible via the header file `<stdlib.h>`. The format of a call to `malloc()` is as follows:

```
void *malloc(size_t);
```

A simple example would be:

```
int ObjectSize, *IntPtr;

IntPtr =  malloc(sizeof(ObjectSize));
```

Here the function returns a void pointer to a piece of memory of size `objectsize`. The void pointer can be assigned to a pointer of any type and if the call fails, e.g. there is insufficient memory to meet the request, then a `null` pointer is returned. Where a request for memory is successful the memory pointed to by the returned pointer will be uninitialized, i.e. it will contain unknown values. This function is typically used in conjunction with the operator `sizeof` which returns the number of bytes required to store an object of the type of its operand. Here is a further simple example:

```
#include <stdlib.h>

Struct Details        /* create a record description  */
{
      char Name[30];
      int Age;
      char Gender;
      float Salary;
};
struct Details *DetailsPtr;
              /* declare a pointer to instances of the records */

DetailsPtr = malloc(sizeof(Details));
```

```
/* get memory for one instance of the structure */
/* type and assign the pointer to that memory to */
/* the struct pointer                            */
```

Releasing dynamically allocated memory

The memory which is allocated at run time comes from a finite heap and unless you, the programmer, explicitly return it back to the heap when you are finished with it, you may easily run out of heap space when performing dynamic calls. There is another function, also available in <stdlib.h>, which gives you the ability to to release memory that you no longer need and this called:

```
void free(void *);
```

This takes a single argument which is a pointer to void, i.e. can be given a pointer of any type. The action of this function is to release the heap memory which its argument points to and return it to the heap.

Any heap memory held by a program will be released when that program terminates, but it is good programming practice to control the allocation and deallocation of run-time memory.

Exercises for dynamic data structures

6.1 Using dynamic memory allocation, write a C program which prompts a user for the number of elements in a linear array, dynamically allocates memory for an array of integers of that dimension and then reads in the values for each element of that array. Your program should then dynamically create a linked list which contains an entry for each unique value in the integer array, and for each such value it should also hold a count of its frequency amongst the values of the elements of the array. At the end of your program the contents of the linked list should be displayed one per line. For example, suppose that there were 7 elements to the array and the values for those elements were

−7 3 3 5 3 5 −7

then your program should display the following:

−7 occurs 2 times
3 occurs 3 times
5 occurs 2 times

6.2 Write a C program which dynamically allocates elements for a doubly linked list containing details of cars. Each element should contain the manufacturer, model, engine capacity and price for a car and, when a new car is added to the list, it should be inserted in order based on

ascending price. A user should be able to move backwards and for-
wards through this list while searching for the car of their choice and
each car should be displayed separately on the screen.

Chapter 7

File input/output using ANSI C

OBJECTIVES

On completion of this chapter you will be able to:

□ use stream-based input/output;

□ use formatted input/output;

□ use character-based input/output;

□ implement direct file input/output on text and binary files using file-positioning functions;

□ rewrite a file *in situ*.

By this point you will already be familiar with many of the input and output functions available for interacting with the standard input (usually keyboard) and the standard output (usually the VDU). We will investigate how the ANSI C standard has provided facilities to handle input and output through a set of libraries. Input and output are not actually part of the C language itself but are provided via a set of standard libraries. The ANSI C standard describes the functions, types and macros that are available through the libraries and included in C programs using the usual `#include` preprocessor command.

The ANSI C standard provides a number of groups of functions – file operations, formatted input and output, character input and output, direct input and output, file-positioning functions and error functions. Around one third of all standard library function prototypes are to be found in `<stdio.h>`, which deals largely with input and output based on streams. A stream is a source or destination of data which can be associated with particular hardware such as a disk, printer etc. The two types of stream are text based (line based – terminated by `\n`) and binary (raw bytes of data). Streams can be associated with a file and we shall see how this can be achieved.

Stream-based input and output

This section introduces the functions based on associating streams with files. We will look at using file i/o to implement a problem solution.

The problem
The following problem will also serve to bring together several of the previously met C constructs and programming techniques.

> *A banking system exists which logs transaction details for customers. Each transaction is described by an integer account number, customer name, integer amount in pounds and float balance. The banking system holds a set of transactions on file. Functions are to be written, one to read the transactions from disk file and one to write transactions to the screen. The function to read the transactions should accept a filename as parameter and place the transactions into a linked list, adding at the head of the list, the head pointer which is provided as a parameter. The function to write the transactions should output from the linked list to the screen, starting at the head. A suitable data structure should be created for the linked list of customer transactions.*
>
> *The data is held in the file as colon separated fields as follows:*

```
account_num:name:amount:balance
```

> *You should create a main program which reads test data from file into the linked list and then displays the data from the linked list on the screen, displaying the number of transactions displayed.*

Structured-English solution
read_transactions
       input file name
       open file
       create new node
       while there are transactions on file
              read a transaction
              place transaction into linked list
              create new node
       end while
       free last created unused node
       close file
       return head pointer

show_transactions
       initialize transaction count
       store head pointer

```
            while pointer not null
                    print contents of list node
                    move to next node
                    increment count
            end while
    return count
```

The program

```c
#include <stdio.h>
#include <stdlib.h>
#include <errno.h>

#define MAX 80

typedef struct transactions{
            int account_num;
            char name[MAX];
            int amount;
            float balance;
            struct transactions *next;
                    } Transnode;

Transnode *read_transactions( Transnode *head, const char *filename)
{
        Transnode *tmp_ptr, *new_trans;
        FILE *fptr;

        if( (fptr = fopen( filename, "r")) == NULL)
        {
                perror("file open");
                exit(0);
        }
        new_trans = malloc( sizeof( Transnode ));
        while( fscanf(fptr, "%d:%[^:]:%d:%f\n",
                &new_trans->account_num, new_trans->name,
            &new_trans->amount,&new_trans->balance) == 4)
        {
                tmp_ptr = head;
                head = new_trans;
                new_trans->next = tmp_ptr;
              new_trans = malloc( sizeof( Transnode ));
        }
        free( new_trans );
        fclose( fptr );
        return( head );
```

Use `typedef` to create a suitable self-referential structure to hold the transactions

```
}

int show_transactions(Transnode *head)
{
        Transnode *tmp_ptr;
        int count = 0;

        tmp_ptr = head;
        while( tmp_ptr )
        {
                printf("%d:%s:%d:%f\n", tmp_ptr->account_num,
                                        tmp_ptr->name,
                                        tmp_ptr->amount,
                                        tmp_ptr->balance);
                tmp_ptr = tmp_ptr->next;
                count++;
        }
        return( count );
}

main()
{
        char filename[MAX];
        Transnode *head = (Transnode *) NULL;
        int count = 0;

        printf("Enter a filename: ");
        scanf("%s",filename);
        head = read_transactions( head, filename );
        count = show_transactions( head );
        printf("\n%d transactions in total\n", count);
        exit(0);
}
```

Now let us examine the structure of the above program with respect to input and ouput.

Using FILE pointers

```
#include <stdio.h>

FILE *fptr;

        if( (fptr = fopen( filename, "r")) == NULL)
        {
                perror("file open");
```

```
                        exit(0);

            }
```

The include file `<stdio.h>` contains the function prototypes, structures and macros necessary for stream-based input and output. Here also is defined a structure which holds information regarding buffer sizes and pointers to manipulate the buffer which is used to block transfer data from storage devices to your program. The details of how this is achieved are not relevant here; what is important is that a pointer to this structure is declared and all the input and output functions then use this pointer to access the data. This is achieved using the `FILE *fptr;` statement. `FILE` is the stream structure and this is associated with a data source or destination using the `fopen()` function.

Notice that on failure, `fopen()` returns a `null` pointer. If you include the header `<errno.h>` then you can call the useful function `perror("identifier");`. This returns a meaningful error pertaining to the last failed library call giving messages such as `file open: file not found` etc.

Notice also the second argument to `fopen()` – `"r"`. This sets up the file for reading. There are a number of possibilities for this parameter summarized below:

`"r"`	Opens file for reading; create if doesn't exist
`"w"`	Opens file for writing – discard previous contents; create if doesn't exist
`"a"`	Opens file to append to; create if doesn't exist
`"r+"`	Opens file for update, reading and writing
`"w+"`	Open new file for update, or discard contents if file already exists
`"a+"`	Open file for appending; create if doesn't exist

The file pointer can now be used to access a data source or destination – in our case we are reading only and from file.

Formatted input and output

```
while( fscanf(fptr, "%d:%%[^:]:%d:%f\n"
        &new_trans->account_num, new_trans->name,
        &new_trans->amount, &new_trans->balance) ==4)
```

The above shows an example of using the file pointer to access the opened file. You have met `scanf()` and `printf()` in previous chapters; here we now have functions from the same family but they are used to access opened files hence `fscanf()` (and `fprintf()`). These functions work in the same way by using format specifiers to format data read or written from/to the stream.

Remember that our specification stated a particular format for the transaction data held on file, which was:

```
int:char_array:int:float
```

which represented :

```
account_num:name:amount:balance
```

In the `scanf()` function call the first parameter is the file pointer, the second parameter is the format specifier and the third and subsequent parameters are the addresses of variables which will be used to hold the read data described by the format specifiers.

Let us look further at the format specifiers: `"%d:%[^:]:%d:%f\n"`

These are interpreted as:

`%d`   read an integer until colon encountered;
`%[^:]`   read characters which do not (^) contain the colon until colon is reached;
`%d`   same again, as above;
`%f\n`   read a float value until new line encountered.

Notice that the variables are ordered such that the correct specifier is applied – this is most important, thus we have:

```
while( fscanf(fptr, "%d:%[^:]:%d:%f\n",
              &new_trans->account_num, new_trans->name,
              &new_trans->amount,&new_trans->balance) == 4)
```

Notice that it is the address of the variables which must be supplied for `fscanf()`, in this case they are fields within the transaction structure. These functions return a value which corresponds to the number of items successfully read (or written in the case of `fprintf()`) and so this allows for error checking. Another useful return value is the constant EOF or 'end of file', so the above could have been written as:

```
while( fscanf(fptr, "%d:%[^:]:%d:%f\n",
              &new_trans->account_num, new_trans->name,
              &new_trans->amount,&new_trans->balance) != EOF)
```

`printf()` and `fprintf()` work in a similar manner but do not require the address of the variables to be written, e.g.

```
printf("%d:%s:%d:%f\n", tmp_ptr->account_num,
                        tmp_ptr->name,
                        tmp_ptr->amount,
                        tmp_ptr->balance);
```

There are many conversion specifiers possible, here are a few of the more common ones:

Conversion character	Argument type
`%d`	Decimal integer
`%i`	Integer in octal or hexadecimal
`%u`	Unsigned decimal integer
`%o` `%x`	Octal or hexadecimal integer
`%f`	Floating point number
`%lf`	Double-precision floating point number
`%c`	Character
`%s`	`null`-terminated string of characters

Refer to your manuals for a fuller description and remember `scanf()` requires pointers, i.e. addresses

Closing the file

```
fclose( fptr );
```

The stream should be closed when no longer required, using the `fclose()` function. The call to `exit()` will also close all opened streams. It should be noted that the number of connected streams is limited for any one running program, depending on your implementation and operating system, typically 20 in total. You can find out the exact number using the constant `FOPEN_MAX` which is defined in `<stdio.h>`. Note also that three streams are preconnected for every running program, `stdin` (standard input – keyboard), `stdout` (standard output – VDU) and `stderr` (standard error – VDU). These constants are defined in the header `<stdio.h>`. The `printf()` function call is equivalent to calling `fprintf(stdout,....)`.

A call to `exit()` requires that you include `<stdlib.h>`.

Language-specific features

String-based formatted input and output

In the same family as `scanf()` and `printf()` there exist the functions `sscanf()` and `sprintf()`. These work in the usual manner except that they take as their source (for `sscanf()`) and destination (for `sprintf()`) character arrays which are `null` terminated, i.e. strings. So for example it may be required that a data packet be produced of a fixed format; this can be achieved with the following type of call:

```
int id,dest;
float amount;
char packet[18];

sprintf(packet,"%5d%7d%5.2f",id, dest,amount);
```

Make sure that you understand how these specifiers work in this example.

Error functions

There are a number of error functions provided by the standard C library and to use them you need to include `<errno.h>`. We have already used the `perror()` function, there are others more specific to file handling. The following is a brief description of these:

- ```
  void perror( const char *str );
  ```

  prints the message pointed to by `str` and an error message dependent on the implementation defined error codes available;
- ```
  int feof( FILE *fptr );
  ```

  returns non-zero if the end of file indicator is set;
- ```
  int ferror( FILE *fptr );
  ```

  returns non-zero if an error has occurred on the stream;
- ```
  void clearerr( FILE *fptr );
  ```

  clears the end of file or error condition, set on the stream.

Exercise on stream input/output

7.1   Write a program that accepts two command line arguments representing file names and appends the second file to the end of the contents of the first. If any error conditions arise then a suitable error message should be output to the user. The files are ASCII files composed of lines of text.

Character based input/output and direct file access in C

The previous section showed how input and output can be achieved using streams. In this section you will meet a set of functions which allow input and output on a character by character basis. The ability to directly manipulate the positioning within a file will also be explored at the same time using an example problem as the vehicle for presenting these facilities in ANSI C.

The problem
The following will present an file encryption program which uses character processing as its basis.

A program is to be written which allows the simple encryption of a text-based document, held in a file.

The program is to accept a filename as a command line argument and then on successfully opening the file, rewrite the same file in situ, *replacing alphabetic upper or lower case characters by characters which have been shifted five places up the ASCII table. Characters at the end of the alphabet are shifted round to the beginning such that, for example, 'Z' becomes 'E' and 'y' becomes 'd'.*

Structured-English solution
open the file
while there are characters to read
        read a character
        if alphabetic character
                unget last character
                find current file position
                reposition for writing
                if uppercase character
                        offset character
                        if character beyond 'Z'
                                wrap around character
                        end if
                else
                        offset character
                        if character beyond 'z'
                                wrap around character
                        end if
                end if
        endif
        overwrite character
        find current file position
        reposition for reading
        end while

The program

```c
#include <stdio.h>
#include <stdlib.h>
#include <ctype.h>
#include <errno.h>

#define OFFSET 5

main (int argc, char *argv[])
{
        FILE *fptr;
        int Charin;
        long file_pos;

        if((fptr = fopen( argv[1], "r+" )) == NULL)
        {
                perror( "file open ");
                exit(0);
        }
        while(( Charin = fgetc( fptr )) != EOF )
```

```
        {
                if( isalpha( Charin ) )
                {
                        ungetc( Charin, fptr );
                        file_pos = ftell( fptr );
                        fseek( fptr, file_pos, SEEK_SET);
                        if( isupper( Charin ))
                        {
                                Charin += OFFSET;
                                if( Charin >= 'Z')
                                        Charin = 'A' + (Charin - 'Z') - 1;
                        }
                        else
                        {
                                Charin += OFFSET;
                                if( Charin >= 'z')
                                        Charin = 'a' + (Charin - 'z') - 1;
                        }
                        fputc( Charin, fptr );
                        file_pos = ftell( fptr );
                        fseek( fptr, file_pos, SEEK_SET );
                }
        }
        fclose( fptr );
}
```

Let us now examine the main features of this program.

Opening a file for update

```
        if((fptr = fopen( argv[1], "r+" )) == NULL)
```

Look up `fflush()` in your manuals for a fuller explanation of this function

Here the mode of opening the file is "r+", which means open the file for updating – reading and writing. In this mode it is the programmer's intention to modify the file *in situ*. Great care must be taken in using this mode of file access when switching between reading a file and writing a file. Before making such a switch one of two functions should be called to update the read and write positions. Either a call to `fflush`(fptr) – which causes all characters buffered in the FILE structure to be sent to disk (flushed) and read/write positions updated, or a call to `fseek()` which repositions the read/write positions – this call will be explored further shortly.

`null` is defined in `stdio.h` and returned if the call to `fopen()` fails.

Character-based input and output

```
        while(( Charin = fgetc( fptr )) ! = EOF )
```

The type of input/output required by this program is 'character-based file i/o', allowing each character in turn to be read, processed and written back to file. `fgetc()` returns the next character pointed at in the stream as an unsigned `char` converted to `int`. `EOF` is returned at end of file.

Character class testing

```
if( isalpha( Charin ));
if( isupper( Charin ));
```

The standard C library provides a useful set of functions which can be used by including the header `<ctype.h>`. These functions take an integer parameter (often the return from the `fgetc()` call) and return non-zero if true and zero otherwise. The above two calls check whether `Charin` is alphabetic (upper or lower case) and whether `Charin` is upper case respectively.

Look up the others in this group of functions, e.g. `isgraph()`, `ispunct()`.

There are also two functions which convert the case of letters, their prototypes are:

```
int toupper(int);
```

and

```
int tolower(int);
```

Direct or random file access

```
ungetc( Charin, fptr );
file_pos = ftell( fptr );
fseek( fptr, file_pos, SEEK_SET);
```

`ungetc()` is a somewhat unusual function and really peculiar to C. However, having said that, it is probably true to say that file handling is very much a language-specific feature for most programming languages, even though the range of functionality is mostly similar. `ungetc()` places a character (actually the character converted to `int`) back onto the stream (into the `FILE` buffering mechanism) so that it will be returned on the next read with `fgetc()`. The ANSI C standard only guarantees that one character can be pushed back per stream, any extra being implementation specific.

Having called this alphabetic value, it is now our intention to overwrite it and to do this requires that the write position be set to just before this returned character. This is achieved using `ftell()`, which returns the current position in the stream (it returns a `long int`) which can in turn then be passed to `fseek()`, which sets the file position for read and write on the stream. The constant `SEEK_SET` signifies that the position is from the beginning of file but MUST be used with `file_pos` which was obtained from a call to `ftell()` as we are using a text file. If a file is opened in binary mode, then `file_pos` can be an actual number of bytes from the start of file (in our case the file was opened in text mode). This allows direct or random-access files (with a suitable hashing algorithm) to be set up (in binary mode) but note

To open in binary mode the mode `"rb+"` would have to be used in the call to `fopen()`. See your manual for details of using binary-mode files.

that, for this to work, the file must contain fixed-format data if a jump to a particular record is to be calculated.

At this point in the program it is now possible to add the offset to the alphabetic character and then overwrite the returned character with the newly transposed one.

Overwriting existing file data

```
fputc( Charin, fptr );
file_pos = ftell( fptr ):
fseek( fptr, file_pos, SEEK_SET );
```

The `fputc()` function writes the transposed character to the stream (file in this case), which, remember, is now set at the position of just before the character originally read untransposed, i.e. overwriting its original value. After this the read position needs to be updated so that the same character is not read again. This is achieved using `ftell()` and `fseek()` in the same manner as previously. The program is now ready to start the loop again and read the next available character.

Language-specific features

Character based input and output functions

So far the functions `fgetc()`, `fputc()` and `ungetc()` have been met. There are several others which will be briefly described now:

Find these macro definitions in your header file – stdio.h, see your manuals for its exact location on your system.

- `int getchar( void );`

  This is actually a macro defined in <stdio.h> and obtains a character (as an `int`) from the standard input (`stdin`).
- `int putchar( int char );`

  This is also a macro defined in <stdio.h> and places a character (as an `int`) onto the standard output stream (`stdout`).
- `int getc( FILE *fptr );`

  `int putc( int char, FILE *fptr );`

  Same as `fgetc()` and `fputc()` except that these are macros which may evaluate stream more than once.
- `char *fgets( char *ch, int n, FILE *fptr );`

  reads at most *n*–1 characters into the array pointed to by `ch`. If a newline character \n is encountered then it is included in the array which is finally terminated by a `null` character \0.
- `int fputs( const char *str, FILE *fptr );`

  writes the string `str` to the stream pointed to by `fptr`, this need not contain the newline character.

Other file-positioning functions

The main file-positioning functions used are `ftell()` and `fseek()`, which have been met already. The following is also available in the standard library:

- `void rewind( FILE *fptr );`

  move to beginning of file, ignoring any error conditions. This is the same as:

  `fseek( fptr, 0L, SEEK_SET ); clearerr( fptr );`

You should also be aware of `getpos()` and `fsetpos()` – look these up. They are less commonly used.

Other file operations

A few more file manipulating routines exist that may be of use:

- `int remove( const char *file_name);`

  removes the file with name `file_name` if it exists and you have the necessary permissions, non-zero being returned on failure;

- `int rename( const char *orig_name, const char *new_name);`

  renames the file from `orig_name` to `new_name`, returning non-zero if an error occurs;

- `FILE *freopen( const char *file_name, const char *mode, FILE *fptr );`

  reopens a file already associated with a stream returning a new `FILE` pointer. Usually used in reassigning the pre-opened streams `stdin`, `stdout` or `stderr`.

Summary for file input and output

- Formatted input and output is achieved using the `printf()` and `scanf()` family of i/o functions. These require the use of format specifiers and the most commonly found are:

Conversion character	Argument type
%d	Decimal integer
%i	Integer in octal or hexadecimal
%u	Unsigned decimal integer
%o %x	Octal or hexadecimal integer
%f	Floating point number
%lf	Double-precision floating point number
%c	Character
%s	`null`-terminated string of characters

`fprintf()` and `fscanf()` can be used to associate streams with files as des-tinations or sources respectively. The file must first be opened and associated with a stream using `fopen()` which requires that a mode be specified as shown in the following table:

"r"	Opens file for reading; create if doesn't exist
"w"	Opens file for writing – discard previous contents,;create if doesn't exist
"a"	Opens file to append to; create if doesn't exist
"r+"	Opens file for update, reading and writing
"w+"	Open new file for update, or discard contents if file already exists
"a+"	Open file for appending; create if doesn't exist

So example usage would look like:

```
FILE *fptr;
    if( (fptr = fopen( filename, "r")) == NULL)
    {
                    perror("file open");
                    exit(0)
    }
    new_trans = malloc( sizeof( Transnode ));
    while( fscanf(fptr, "%d:%[^:]:%d:%f\n",
            &new_trans->account_num, new_trans->name,
            &new_trans->amount,&new_trans->balance) ==4)
            printf("%d:%s:%d:%f\n", tmp_ptr->account_num,
                                    tmp_ptr->name,
                                    tmp_ptr->amount,
                                    tmp_ptr->balance);
```

There also exist string formatting functions `sscanf()` and `sprintf()` which use a string array as source and destination respectively.

- Character based input and output using files is achieved using `fgetc()` and `fputc()`, e.g.

```
while(( Charin = fgetc( fptr )) ! = EOF )
```

and

fputc(Charin, fptr);

- Direct file access is possible using the functions `ftell()` and `fseek()`, which when used in conjunction with `fgetc()` and `ungetc()` can allow files opened in update mode to be rewritten *in situ*,e.g.

```
ungetc( Charin, fptr );             /* return character to stream*/
file_pos - ftell( fptr );           /* find current file position*/
fseek( fptr, file_pos, SEEK_SET); /* set write position to
```

```
                                       overwrite*/
fputc( Charin, fptr );               /*overwrite character*/
file_pos = ftell( fptr );            /*find current file position*/
fseek( fptr, file_pos, SEEK_SET);    /* set read position for next*/
                                     /* character in file file*/
```

- There exist several other file handling functions e.g.

  `int remove( const char *file_name);` removes a file;

  `int rename( const char *orig_name, const char *new_name);` renames a file;

  `FILE *freopen( const char *file_name, const char *mode, FILE *fptr );` reassigns a stream to an existing one.

Exercise on character based i/o and direct access

7.2   A program is to be written that reads in a single word as a string from the user and the name of a text file containing some normal English text. The file is searched for all occurrences of the word (case sensitive) and replaces these words *in situ* with the correct number of 'X' characters such that all occurrences of that word are blanked out by X's. Note that the word is to be blanked even if embedded in a longer word, e.g. 'any' in 'anything' results in "XXXthing".

Chapter 8

C as a base for other programming techniques

OBJECTIVES

On completion of this chapter you will be able to:

- □ define object-oriented programming;

- □ specify the facilities required in a programming language to support object-oriented programming;

- □ migrate to the C++ programming language;

- □ define the sort of extensions provided by the Concurrent C programming language;

- □ explain how processes can be created and communicate both asynchronously and synchronously.

C forms the basis of several extended languages developed for use in different programming styles, notably C++ for the object-oriented approach and Concurrent C for parallel/multiprocessing problems. This chapter gives a very brief introduction to these evolving programming paradigms and indicates how C has been extended to support their distinctive features.

Object-oriented programming (OOP) and C++

Notwithstanding the criticisms of many language purists that extending a language designed originally in the early 1970s for use in a paradigm devised in the early 1980s, C++ looks to be a strong candidate for the industry standard object-oriented programming language.

Object-oriented programming

In procedural or imperative-style programming the approach to problem solving is typically process or data oriented with functional decomposition often being used. This top-down design process evolves a solution by splitting the original problem into subproblems and then repeatedly subdividing each subproblem until it becomes easily solvable. Such solutions are usually highly individual and the ability to reuse components of one problem within another problem is very limited.

Solutions derived using the procedural approach often obscure the mapping between the real-world elements of the original problem and their representation within the implementation. From a maintenance viewpoint, it would be much cleaner if programmers could easily locate these real-world elements within the code. In fact, isolating them also increases the element of control over them and access to them by programmers, another good programming practice.

Having introduced several drawbacks of the procedural paradigm, let us consider OOP and how it attempts to tackle these problems.

Objects, classes and C++

From the name you might guess that OOP is concerned with objects, in particular real-world objects and their representation within the implementation. So perhaps the first question to ask is what is an object?

In the real world objects are often physical things such as bank accounts, people, stores' items and so forth. Representing such things in code is quite simply the use of a user-defined type to describe the attributes of such physical things. Thus a bank account may be characterized by its type (deposit, current), the balance, the interest rate available, the minimum balance, a list of transactions and so on. This would be a `struct` in C, i.e.

```
struct BankAccount
{
        enum AccountType    Account;
        double CurrentBalance  ;
        float MinBalance;
        struct TransActions * TransPtr;
};
```

However, in real life a bank account is given meaning by being acted upon; the holder may deposit or withdraw money, request the current balance, request the list of previous transactions etc. So a real-world object is really the data characterizing that object and the operations which can be performed on that data. Hence in the OOP paradigm an object is both the data and the operations on that data. In OOP parlance such operations are called methods.

In order to support this concept of an object, C is extended such that it contains a structure called a `class`. At its simplest a `class` is really a `struct` with the facility to describe functions. As was indicated earlier, making objects completely separate from each other has implications about the scope of the data and functions described within. In C++ by default all the data and functions within a class are private, i.e. the data in one object can only be modified or seen by the functions in that object. However, reality occasionally intrudes and it is necessary to let other objects know what functions are available for use within an object. After all, how else are objects to communicate with each other?

Encapsulation and data hiding

The concepts of encapsulation and data hiding are concerned with restricting access to data. One of the problems of unrestricted data access is that all data is available to and modifiable by all parts of a program. Through the derivation of abstract data types, in which data structures and the procedures that operate on them are separated out into distinct program parts or modules (cf. Modula-2, Ada), data hiding and encapsulation become possible. Data hiding is the process of ensuring that only those parts of an abstract data type which must be made known to the rest of the program are made visible and the remainder are kept hidden. Encapsulation is the process whereby a distinct boundary is created between different abstractions to ensure the integrity of the data structures held in each abstraction, i.e. no procedure in one abstraction can access the data of another. Such a distinct boundary has to be explicitly supported in the implementation language, e.g. modules in Modula-2, tasks in Ada, classes in Eiffel.

A simple example of this could be the concept of a library which has books and borrowers. The data abstraction for the books could be an array of `struct`s holding the title, author, ISBN, classification, due date, fine rate and whether a book is on loan. To control access to this array there might be only five procedures required, namely to issue a book, to return a book, to add a new book, to delete a book and to display a book. Only these procedures would be made visible to the rest of the program, the array of books being kept hidden. These would form one module and the only way any change to the array of books could be made is by invoking one of these five procedures. The borrowers might themselves form another abstraction which is also an array of `struct`s holding the details of each borrower. A set of operations on that array might be to add a borrower, to delete a borrower, to display a borrower, to borrow a book and to bring a book back. It should be clear that action of borrowing a book on the part of a borrower should have an effect on the array of book details, but the only way that the borrower abstraction procedure 'borrow a book' can alter the array of books is to invoke the book abstraction procedure 'issue a book'.

In Modula-2 or Ada each abstract data type comprises two entities, a definition file and an implementation file. The definition file is a description of those aspects of the abstract data type which the rest of the world needs to know, e.g. data types and function prototypes. The implementation file contains the actual code for those function prototypes (and possibly others). This separation means that data encapsulation and data hiding are supported to a very strong degree.

C++ has an added user-defined data-typing mechanism, the `class`, which supports the explicit separation of those data and methods (or functions) which other classes need to know about and the data and functions which are private to the class. Such classes can be placed in a single source-code file, but this would seem to lose some of the possible parallel team-based development which might be required for large projects. An alternative would be to use the separate compilation facility supported by C++ and use header files and code files (as discussed earlier in Chapter 3) to achieve a situation similar to that of Modula-2 or Ada. Thus, although C++ does not enforce the use of the header and code file approach, the latter is very strongly recommended.

Now it has been seen that C++ incorporates support for the concept of class, what other capabilities does a class bestow? Another important aspect of OOP is the idea of inheritance.

Inheritance and C++

Inheritance is a particularly powerful mechanism for enabling the reuse of existing software. The basic idea is that of a hierarchy where the most general form of an object is placed towards the top and the most specific forms are found at the lowest level (the leaves of a tree structure). Within the hierarchy each child inherits all the data and operations of its parent and it can add to or amend these.

Using our bank account example, there is a possible hierarchy with suggested data and operations associated with each node or class. Let's assume that a particular bank has three types of accounts, namely a current account, a deposit account and a special form of deposit account called an high-interest account. For all accounts, regardless of type, the bank holds the name of the customer, a unique account number, the branch number and the current balance. Again for all accounts, customers can deposit money into an account and they can also request a statement of their last 20 transactions. Customers with current accounts can also withdraw money so long as a minimum balance of 50 pounds is retained. They can also request to see the current balance. Customers with deposit accounts are given interest on the money they deposit, the rate being 7.4%. Consequently they can request to see a statement of the interest earned to date. They can also withdraw cash and when this is done the current balance is increased by the interest earned to date, the withdrawal debited from this figure and the balance becomes the current balance. For the high-interest account the interest rate is 14.2%, but the interest is not added to the account until the end of each financial year, a maximum of four withdrawals in a twelve-month period are allowed and the amount withdrawn cannot exceed 10% of the principal interest. Any withdrawal is debited from the principal.

Here is the simple hierarchy for this:

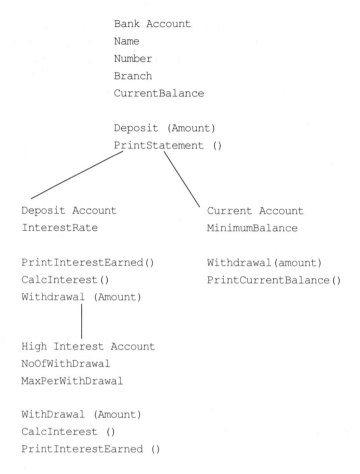

```
                        Bank Account
                        Name
                        Number
                        Branch
                        CurrentBalance

                        Deposit (Amount)
                        PrintStatement ()



    Deposit Account                   Current Account
    InterestRate                      MinimumBalance


    PrintInterestEarned()             Withdrawal(amount)
    CalcInterest()                    PrintCurrentBalance()
    Withdrawal (Amount)



    High Interest Account
    NoOfWithDrawal
    MaxPerWithDrawal


    WithDrawal (Amount)
    CalcInterest ()
    PrintInterestEarned ()
```

Notice how in the hierarchy those things which are common to all the accounts are allocated to the node or class Bank Account from which all other account types inherit either directly, Deposit Account, or indirectly, High Interest Account. Isolating or abstracting these common features into a separate class allows us to reuse them However, the inheritance concept really says that, if one class inherits from another, then everything in the parent class can be considered as part of the child class; there is no need to redefine all of those features. This means that the child only needs to define those features which make it different or distinguish it from its parent.

Thus in our example since Bank Account contains all the common features, Current Account inherits these and defines only extra operations which distinguish it from a generic account. Inheritance passes through classes at different levels, i.e. the class High Interest Account inherits from the Deposit Account, but it also inherits from Bank Account since Deposit Account inherits from Bank Account.

This aspect of an inheritance hierarchy really comprises two levels of abstraction; abstraction within the particular problem, i.e. the creation of the Bank Account class, and abstraction across problems, i.e. is there a more generic form of account, which is a base description of bank accounts, building society accounts, post office accounts and so forth. The success of class reuse depends upon the abstraction activity and one of the common coding needs is for a piece of code that is like some existing code but different in a number of ways. This would fall nicely into the parent/child inheritance relationship.

One facet that has not been discussed is the case where a child class inherits something from its parent class, but it either does not want it or needs to apply different rules. Well, within inheritance a child can redefine operations inherited from a parent and such redefinition can ensure that either the body of the operation is blank or it has completely different code. An example from the hierarchy above would be the `Withdrawal (Amount)` operation as shown against the `Deposit Account` and `High Interest Account` classes. Both classes allow withdrawal but the actions taken for a withdrawal on a `Deposit Account` differ from those for a withdrawal on a `High Interest Account`. Hence the `High Interest Account class` redefines the `Withdrawal(Amount)` operation which it inherits from the `Deposit Account class`. This is an example of polymorphism.

Polymorphism and C++

This very grandiose name means the capability of having one name with many forms or, in OOP terms, one operation which can be applied to many different objects and, though the spirit of the operation is maintained, the actual actions may differ. Although this is somewhat confusing, let's see if an example can help. One very useful debugging aid would be the ability for each object to print out the values of its internal data. Now if we look at the `Bank Account` hierarchy, we can see that `Bank Account` has four variables, `Deposit Account` has one and `High Interest Account` has two, so that printing out the values for a `High Interest Account` really means print `NoOfWithdrawals` and `MaxWithdrawAmount`, then print the `Deposit Account` data. Printing the `Deposit Account` data means print the `InterestRate` and then print the `Bank Account` data and so forth. Thus each class would have its own version of print and, while the intention of this operation would be to display the data for that object, the actions concerned would differ in each case. This is one form of polymorphism and C++ supports this; it is called function name overloading.

A second form of polymorphism, which most programmers have met and used many times, is called operator overloading. How often have you used statements of the form

```
Result = 1 + 2;
RealResult = 1.0 + 2.0;
```

Here the same symbol '+' is used to perform two quite distinct computing operations, integer and real-number addition. If you consider the difference in the way integers and reals are represented within the computer you should realize that very different low-level code will be involved for the different representations. The compiler recognizes the context in which the '+' occurs and ensures that the correct code is included. This operator overloading is frequently used in C, e.g. the comparison operators, the `&` operator etc. In C the language fixes the overloading, although you, the programmer, must know how to use the overloaded operator.

C++ allows you, the programmer, to explicitly overload existing operators. Why would you want to do this? Looking back at our bank account example, one quite simple way of adding or withdrawing money from an account would be to just use the addition or subtraction operator for these purposes. Thus we could add to the `Bank Account class` the overloaded operator and thus allow statements of the form

```
print ("New Balance = %f\n", MyCurrentAcc += 1000.0)
```

assuming the operator `+=` was defined as returning a `float`.

A simple object-oriented example

Having given a very brief introduction to OOP and C++, here is small example and solution.

In a particular library the following information is held for each book: the author, title, ISBN, unique reference number and shelf number. In this library books are either reference books and cannot be borrowed, or lending books which can be borrowed by the public. Reference books are subdivided into almanacs, atlases, dictionaries and encyclopaedias. Books for loan are subdivided into fiction and non-fiction. Any book available for loan requires information concerning the length of a loan, what fine rate is to be applied, an indicator showing whether the book is on loan. There also must be facilities for issuing, returning, calculating potential fines and associating a book with a specific borrower. Books in the fiction category are classified as one of thriller, sci-fi, adventure or love story . Non-fiction books are categorized by their dewey decimal number. The details about any book in the library should be available for display at any time.

Using inheritance, create a hierarchy to represent this information and then devise appropriate C++ classes to implement that hierarchy.

One solution to the library problem
A graphical illustration of a possible solution is:

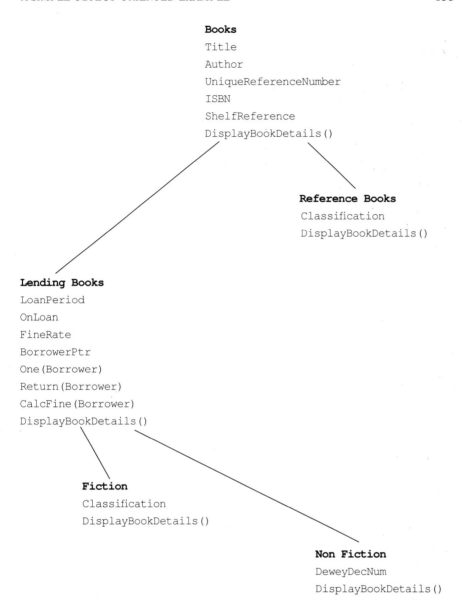

```
Books
Title
Author
UniqueReferenceNumber
ISBN
ShelfReference
DisplayBookDetails()
```

```
Reference Books
Classification
DisplayBookDetails()
```

```
Lending Books
LoanPeriod
OnLoan
FineRate
BorrowerPtr
One(Borrower)
Return(Borrower)
CalcFine(Borrower)
DisplayBookDetails()
```

```
Fiction
Classification
DisplayBookDetails()
```

```
Non Fiction
DeweyDecNum
DisplayBookDetails()
```

The program

This hierarchy can be implemented in C++ in the following way. We are deliberately choosing to use the convention of creating a definition file (a header file containing function prototypes and variables) and an implementation file (containing the code bodies of the function prototypes).

```
// header file for the class Books
// file Books.h

class Books
```

```cpp
{
private:
        char *Title;
        long int RefNumber;
        char *Author;
        unsigned long int ISBN;
        float ShelfRef;
public:
        void DisplayBookDetails(void);
};


// end of Books.h


// source file Books.cpp


#include "Books.h"


void Books::DisplayBookDetails(void)
{
        cout << "Title " << Title << endl;
        cout << "Author " << Authr << endl;
        cout << "ISBN " << ISBN << endl;
        cout << "Shelf Reference " << endl;
}


//end of Books.cpp
```

```cpp
//Header file for RefBooks.h


enum RefTyp = {Almanac, Atlas, Dictionary, Encyclopaedia};
class RefBooks : public Books
{
private:
        enum RefType BookType;
public:
        void DisplayBookDetails(void);
};
// end of RefBooks.h


//source file for RefBooks.cpp


#include "RefBooks.h"


void RefBooks::DisplayBookDetails()
```

```
{
        char *PrintName;

        switch (BookType)
        {
                case Almanac : { PrintName = "Almanac ";
                        break;
                        }
                case Atlas : { PrintName = "Atlas ";
                        break;
                        }
                case Dictionary : { PrintName = "Dictionary ";
                        break;
                        }
                case Encyclopaedia : { PrintName = "Encyclopaedia ";
                        break;
                        }
                default : { PrintName = "Undefined Reference Type ";
                        break:
                        }
        }
        Books::DisplayBookDetails();
        cout << " Reference Book : Type " << PrintName << endl;
}

// end of RefBooks.cpp
```

```
// header file for LendingBooks.h

class LendingBooks : public Books
{
private:
        int LendingPeriod;
        int OnLoan;
        float FineRate;
        class Borrower BorrowerPtr;
public:
        void DisplayBookDetails();
};
// end of LendingBooks.h

//source foe LendingBooks.cpp

#include "LendingBooks.h"
```

```
void LendingBooks::DisplayBookDetails()
{
        Books::DisplayBookDetails();
        cout << "Lending Book." << endl;
        cout << "Loan Period " << LoanPeriod << " days" <<endl;
        cout << "Book on loan " << (OnLoan ? "Yes" : "No") << endl;
        cout << "Fine Rate "<< FineRate << endl;
}

// end of LendingBooks.cpp
```

```
//header file for Fiction.h

enum FictionTypes = {Thriller, Scifi, Adventure, LoveStory};

class Fiction : public LendingBooks
{
private:
        enum FictionType FictionClass;
public:
        void DisplayBookDetails(void);
};
//end of fiction.h

//source file for Fiction.cpp

#include "Fiction.h"

void Fiction::DisplayBookDetails(void)
{
        char *PrintName;

        LendingBooks::DisplayBookDetails();
        switch (FictionClass)
        {
                case Thriller : { PrintName = "Thriller ";
                        break;
                        }
                case Scifi : { PrintName = "Scifi ";
                        break;
                        }
                case Adventure : { PrintName = "Adventure ";
                        break;
                        }
```

```
              case LoveStory : { PrintName = "LoveStory ";
                        break;
                        }
              default : {PrintName = "Unclassified Fiction Book ";
                        break;
                        }
        }
        cout << "Fiction classification " << PrintName << endl;
}
//end of Fiction.cpp
```

```
//header file for NonFiction.h

class NonFiction : public LendingBooks
{
private:
        float DeweyDecNum;
public:
        void DisplayBookDetails(void);
};
//end of NonFiction.h

// source file for NonFiction.cpp

#include "NonFiction.h"

void NonFiction::DisplayBookDetails(void)
{
        LendingBooks::DisplayBookDetails();
        cout << "NonFiction DeweyDecimal Classification";
        cout << DeweyDecNum << endl;
}
// end of NonFiction.cpp
```

Let's examine one or two salient features of this program.

The use of the `private:` and `public:` reserved words

As indicated earlier, one feature of OOP is the facility to hide data from the view of all other objects in a system and to allow it to be manipulated only by the object which contains it. The `private:` reserved word here is an explicit statement that the data listed under that heading is only visible to the object which contains it. Every instance (variable declared to be of type `Books`) of the class `Books` will have its own set of the data. The `public:` reserved word introduces those items, data or methods (functions) which all other objects can see and therefore can use. Thus any object of class `Books` can be told to invoke its `DisplayBookDetails()` method. The manner of invocation is normally called message passing, i.e. another object sends a message to an object of class 'Books' telling it to apply a 'public' method.

Some i/o in C++

```
cout << "Title " << Title << endl;
```

This line shows a typical output line in C++. The function `printf()` can also be used but the messages `cout` and `cin` together with the redirection operators << and >> are the usual i/o facilities in C++. Notice that there is no attempt to distinguish between the type of the values to be printed, i.e. the string "`Title`" and the char pointer variable `Title` are just built up into one sequence. This works because the redirection operator << has been over-loaded so that it can work with any of the base data types. Thus, the compiler knows which of the possible sets of actions associated with << to invoke for each of the operands. The `endl` at the end of the sequence is one of several manipulators and it flushes the output buffer and inserts a carriage return line feed into the output sequence.

The scoping operator

```
void Books :: DisplayBookDetails();
```

This operator is used to indicate that some code or function call is to be resolved by reference to a particular scope. If you examine the statement in the box above, then the scoping operator '::' is used to indicate that the function being defined is to be taken as being within the scope of the class `Books`, i.e. there is a method called `DisplayBookDetails()` in that class. The same operator is used when you need to refer to a method or function which has a name common to both message sender and message receiver. For example, in the classes `Books` and `LendingBooks` there is a method called `DisplayBookDetails()`, though each method has different actions. The body of the code for that method in class `LendingBooks` refers to the method `DisplayBookDetails()` in the class `Books` by explicitly using the scope operator as follows:

```
Books::DisplayBookDetails();
```

Review of C++

This section has given a very brief introduction to OOP and the extensions to C that create the language C++. This has by no means been either a complete or a detailed presentation of either the language or the programming approach and you are referred to other books which are concerned solely with these topics for more detailed information. Of the examples given above you should be aware that i/o can be dealt with in several different ways, that inheritance can be more complex (specifically multiple inheritance can be used) and that in-line expansion of methods can be utilized.

This synopsis is intended to whet your appetite for extended reading about OOP and C++ and to this end you should look for information on the proposed ANSI standard for the C++ language.

The Concurrent C programming language

This is another superset of the C programming language that provides facilities for dealing with multiple processes which run concurrently either on a single central processor or in a truly parallel manner on multiple processors, which can be on the same computer or distributed over several computers. Concurrent C also works with C++ and provides a compile-time option to deal with this. Concurrent languages are particularly elegant in dealing with situations where there are many Concurrent events, such as in real-time systems, operating systems and databases. The language allows problems to be solved in parallel algorithms, which are explicitly coded.

If multiprocessor architectures are to be used, then it becomes essential to use a language which supports parallel flow control, process communication and synchronization. It is possible to use sequential C and encode the concurrency and communication using system calls as would be found under the UNIX operating system, but this requires much work and can lead to non-portable code. We will present only a few of the more salient features of Concurrent C just to give you a flavour for what can be achieved and maybe encourage you to seek further knowledge about this programming paradigm.

Processes

A number of processes make up a Concurrent C program. Each process has its own resources in terms of memory, stack and so forth. As already mentioned, each process may be using the same processor (and thus be scheduled) or may be using multiple processors.

Let us now look at a simple program in Concurrent C:

```
#include <stdio.h>

process spec hello( int ident);
process body hello( id )
{
        printf("Hello World from process %d\n", ident);
}

main()
{
```

```
process hello h0, h1, h2;

printf("Main process starting\n");
h0 = create hello(0);
h1 = create hello(1);
h2 = create hello(2);
printf("Main process terminating");
}
```

If this program is executed the following output is typical:

Main process starting
Hello from process 0
Main process terminating
Hello from process 1
Hello from process 2

Process definition

```
process spec hello( int ident);
process body hello( id )
{
        printf("Hello World from process %d\n", ident);
}
```

Notice that there are two parts to the process template, a specification (spec) and a body. This is to allow large scale software teamwork, so that a process can be specified and used without needing to know how it works, i.e. its implementation. Notice that this looks very much like a function and has parameters, and just like a function, no code is executed until it is called.

Process creation

```
process hello h0, h1, h2;

h0 = create hello( 0 );
```

h0, h1, h2 are variables of type process hello and will hold the returned unique value from a call to create, which brings the new process into existence. It is only now that an instantiation of the process template comes into existence as a new process running concurrently with the main() program. The hello process will output its message to the screen and then terminate. Similarly for the second and third instantiations of the hello process. The main() program itself will terminate on reaching its end. One crucial factor to consider now is time, as we cannot predict when each will be scheduled and in fact execute. We may find that the second hello process runs before main() outputs its termination message. We may even predict that the message will be intertwined and thus garbled. However, most printf() calls are implemented in an atomic manner so that multiple execution of printf() does not occur.

Process communication and transaction calls

One important aspect of concurrency is the ability of processes to interact; these are known as transactions. The model used is that of client–server. A client makes a call to the server. At this point there are two possible interactions – synchronous and asynchronous. In a synchronous interaction the client waits until a reply is received from the server before continuing execution – there is two-way communication. In an asynchronous interaction the client does not wait for a reply and continues execution. The onus is on the server to define the transaction call, e.g.

```
process spec hello(int ident)
{
        trans void print(char *message);
};
```

This specifies that the `hello` process can accept a transaction of type `print` with a pointer to `char` parameter and returns nothing to the caller. Let us look at a modification of our original program to illustrate the transaction.

```
#include <stdio.h>

process spec hello(int ident)
{
        trans void print(char * message);
};
process body hello(id)
{
        while(1)
        {
                accept print(message)
                {
                        printf("Message from process %d is %s\n",
                                        ident, message);
                }
        }
}

main()
{
        process hello h0, h1, h2;

        printf("Main process starting\n");
        h0 = create hello(0);
        h1 = create hello(1);
        h2 = create hello(2);
```

```
h0.print("Hello there");
h1.print("Hello there");
h2.print("Hello there");
printf("Main process terminating");
}
```

Declaring a transaction

```
trans void print(char * message);
```

This is included in the body of the process specification and states that the process will act as a server for a transaction call. In this case the transaction is called `print` and when called by the client (in our case `main()`) can pass a message via the parameter `message` from the client to the server. In this case there is no return value to the client.

Synchronous communication

```
accept print(message)
        {
        printf("Message from process %d is %s\n", ident,
                                        message);
        }
```

In the server a call is made to accept the transaction and results in an output of the form:

Message from process 0 is Hello there

In our case this sits in an infinite loop waiting for clients to initiate a transaction.

Calling the transaction

```
h0 = create hello(0);
h0.print("Hello there");
```

After the new process has been instantiated, the transaction is called by the `main()` program to set up the synchronous transaction. This results in waiting until the server accepts the transaction. In this way processes can synchronize data transfer. This is analogous to the ADA rendezvous, another Concurrent programming language which you may have met. The result is that each new `hello` process receives a message from the `main()` program via this synchronous transaction.

Review of Concurrent C

You have been introduced to a small subset of the Concurrent C programming language. In order to appreciate its uses you will need a knowledge of some real-time and Concurrent systems and be aware of issues such as deadlock and resource starvation. If you are interested in real-time systems or operating system architecture then you will find Concurrent C an excellent way to implement many of the concepts in these areas and you can thus extend your experience of C .

Answers to selected exercises

Chapter 1

1.2
The following program shows how the backslash is used to escape the usual meaning of the " character:

```
#include <stdio.h>
main()
{
        printf("Like this:\"");
        return(0);
}
```

1.2
The program:

```
#include <stdio.h>
main()
{
        printf("Hello ");
        printf("World\n");
        return(0);
}
```

will output:

Hello World

all on one line as the first `printf()` has no newline `\n` character. The cursor will be left on the following line as the second `printf()` contains the newline character.

1.3
The following program shows the sort of use of `printf()` for writing very long lines; simply split them up and insert only the newline character `\n` at the end of lines:

```
#include <stdio.h>
main()
{
        printf("This is a very long line");
        printf("of output which also incorporates");
        printf("the \nprintable character \"");
        printf("as part of its content.\n);
        return(0);
}
```

1.4

Using an editor, look at the header files `<limits.h>` and `<float.h>` usually found in a directory called /usr/include. Look at your manuals for their exact location. Can you see the constants relating to these limits?

For the compiler used by the author these ranges are to be found in the include file `<limit.h>` and they are:

int	=	−32767 ... 32767
float	=	1.175494351e–38 ... 3.402823466e+38
double	=	2.2250738585072014e-308 ... 1.7976931348623158e308
short	=	−32767 ... 32767
long	=	−2147483647 ... 2147483647

The values given for the float and double ranges are the largest and smallest values which can be represented in those data types.

1.5

```
#include <stdio.h>

main()
{
        printf("\n\nint\tfloat\tdouble\tshort\tchar\tlong\n");
        printf("___\t_____\t_____\t_____\t_____\t_____\n");
        printf("%3d\t%5d\t%6d\t%5d\t%4d\t%4d\n\n", sizeof(int),
                                   sizeof(float), sizeof(double),
                                   sizeof(short), sizeof(char),
                                   sizeof(long));
        return(0);
}
```

On the compiler used by the author, Microsoft QuickC, this program produces the following result:

int	float	double	short	char	long
2	4	8	2	1	4

1.6

```
#include <stdio.h>

main()
{
        char Character;
        int Offset;

        printf("\n\nEnter the character and the offset       > ");
        scanf("%c%d", &Character, &Offset);
        printf("\n\nOriginal\tOffset\tTransposed\n");
        printf("_____\t_____\t_____\n");
        printf("%8c\t%6d\t%9c\n\n", Character, Offset,
                                        Character + Offset);
        return(0);
}
```

This solution only answers the first part of this question, i.e. it adds an offset to a given character. You should be able to determine a way of extending this solution to cope with the suggested extra part to this question.

1.7

```
#include <stdio.h>

main()
{
        char Character;

        printf("\n\nEnter a character ..  > ");
        scanf("%c%", &Character);
        printf("%8c is at position %d in the ASCII sequence\n\n",
                    Character, Character);
        return(0);
}
```

This question is intended to make sure that you recognize possible interchangeability of `char` and `int` variables. You should also begin to be aware that in C it is common to embed statements within other statements, e.g. the values which are used to replace the format specifiers in the `printf` statement can be literal values, variables or the result of an expression.

Chapter 2

2.1

The `switch` statement can only be used where the expression which is to be evaluated for the `switch` will produce an integral expression. Where this expression produces a non-integral result the `if...else if` statement must be used. There are other constraints on the use of the `switch` statement, in particular it is not possible to allow the use of ranges for each of the `case` parts as is possible in Pascal, e.g.

```
switch (Value)
{
        case 100..200 :
```

This is not allowed in C. Each possible value must be listed individually; thus the range 100...200 would need to be described as:

```
switch (Value)
{
        case 100:
        case 101:
        case 102:
```

and so on.

2.2

```
#define UpperBound 10000
#define MiddleBound 7500
#define LowMidBound 5000
#define LowerBound 3000

#include <stdio.h>

main()
{
    int Cash;

    printf("\n\nHow much cash do you have to spend on a car ..> ");
    scanf("%d", &Cash);

    if (Cash >= UpperBound)
    {
            printf("\n\n\tConsult Classic Cars Magazine\n\n");
    }
    else if ((Cash < UpperBound) && (Cash >= MiddleBound))
```

```
        {
              printf("\n\nTry an Escort, Sierra, Cavalier or
                                          Rover\n\n");
        }
        else if ((Cash < MiddleBound) && (Cash >= LowMidBound))
        {
              printf("\n\n\tTry a Metro, Maestro, Fiesta or
                                          Astra\n\n");
        }
        else if ((Cash < LowMidBound) && (Cash >= LowerBound))
        {
              printf("\n\n\tTry a Yugo or a Lada\n\n");
        }
        else
        {
              printf("\n\n\tYou cannot buy a new car.\n\n");
        }
        return(0);
}
```

In this example we do not use the `switch` construct because the type of tests we are applying relate to ranges of values, i.e. we are looking to see if the value read in lies between several pairs of bounds. In order to do this using the `switch` we would need to explicitly state all the possible values between each bound and associate one set of actions with them, e.g.

```
switch (Cash)
{
        case 3000:
        case 3001:
        case 3002:

                .        .

        case 4999: {printf("\n\n\tTry a Yugo or a Lada\n\n");
                       break;
                    }
```

2.3
```
#include <stdio.h>

main()
{
    int Choice;

    printf("\n\n\t1 - Pride and Prejudice\n");
    printf("\t2 - Palgrave's Golden Treasury\n");
```

```
    printf("\t3 - ANSI C Standard\n");
    printf("\t4 - English Oxford Dictionary\n\n");

    printf("\t\tPlease choose a book ..> ");
    scanf("%d", &Choice);

    switch(Choice)
    {
        case 1 : {printf("\n\nYou are a lover of English h
                                    Literature\n\n");
              break;
            }
        case 2 : {printf("\n\nYou like Poetry\n\n");
              break;
            }
        case 3 : {printf("\n\nYou like manuals\n\n");
              break;
            }
        case 4 : {printf("\n\nYou are a seeker of knowledge\n\n");
              break;
            }
        default: {printf("\n\nNo such option, please try
                                    again\n\n");
              break;
            }
    }
    return(0);
}
```

Here we use the `switch` statement to check the value of the option chosen by the user. This value is expected to be an integer and is read into the program using the `scanf` function. Note that the argument for the format specifier in the `scanf` function must be an address and that the address of the argument is obtained by applying the `adress` operator `&` to the variable name, i.e. `&Choice`.

2.4

```
#define FridayFare          26.00
#define OtherDayFare        FridayFare * 0.80
#define StudentRate         0.75
#define SeniorCitizenRate   0.67

#include <stdio.h>

main ()
```

```
{
        float Fare;
        char Student;
        char SeniorCitizen;
        char ReturnKey;
        int Day = 0;

                printf ("Intended day of travel:- \n\n");
                printf ("\t1 - Monday\n\t2 - Tuesday\n");
                printf ("\t3 - Wednesday\n\t4 - Thursday\n");
                printf ("\t5 - Friday\n\t6 - Saturday\n");
                printf ("\t7 - Sunday\n\nEnter a number ..> ");
                scanf ("%d", &Day);
                ReturnKey = getchar();/* remove the carriage return
                                        from the previous input.*/
                printf ("\n\nAre you a student [Y/N] ..> ");
                scanf ("%c", &Student);
                ReturnKey = getchar();
                printf ("\n\nAre you a senior citizen [Y/N] ..> ");
                scanf ("%c", &SeniorCitizen);

                switch (Day)
                {
                        case 1:
                        case 3:
                        case 4:
                        case 6:
                        case 7: { Fare = OtherDayFare;
                                break;
                                }
                        case 5: { Fare = FridayFare;
                                break;
                                }
                        default: { printf ("\nInvalid value given for
                                                day\n");
                                Fare = 0.0;
                                break;
                                }
                }

                if (( Student == 'Y') || ( Student == 'y'))
                {
                        Fare = Fare * StudentRate;
                }
                else if (( SeniorCitizen == 'Y') || ( SeniorCitizen
                                                == 'y'))
```

```
                {
                        Fare = Fare * SeniorCitizenRate;
                }
                printf ("\n\nThe cost of your ticket will be %6.2f
                                                \n\n", Fare);


                return (0);
}
```

We can use the `switch` statement to check which day of the week has been given because the value entered is an integer. If the variable `Day` has a value of 1, 2, 3, 4, 6 or 7 then the same block of code is executed. Notice that the code checks for the possibility of a lower or upper case `Y` as input. Finally, make sure that you understand the format specifier `%6.2f` – this is a floating-point format which states that the value is to be displayed in a field six columns wide and with two places after the decimal point.

2.5

```
#include <stdio.h>
#include <ctype..h>

main ()
{
        int UpperLetters = 0, LowerLetters = 0, Digits = 0, Space = 0,
                        Control = 0, Punctuation = 0;
        char Letter;
        int ReturnKey;
        int NumLetters, Count;
        float RealCount;

        printf ("\n\nStarting the character analysis program\n\n");
        printf ("How many characters are to be entered ..>");
        scanf ("%d", &NumLetters);
        ReturnKey = getchar();
        printf ("\n\nEnter the letters :- \n\n");
        for (Count = 0; Count < NumLetters; Count++)
        {
                scanf ("%c", &Letter);
                if (isupper(Letter))
                {
                ++UpperLetters;
                }
                else if (islower(Letter))
                {
                ++LowerLetters;
```

```
          }
          else if (isdigit(Letter))
          {
          ++Digits;
          }
          else if (isspace(Letter))
          {
          ++Space;
          }
          else if (iscntrl(Letter))
          {
          ++Control;
          }
          else if (ispunct(Letter))
          {
          ++Punctuation;
          }
     }
     printf("\n\nCount = %d\n\n",Count);
     printf("\n\nThe analysis of the input is as follows:-
                                        \n\n");

     printf("Uppercase\tLowercase\tDigits\tSpace\tControl\
                                        tPunctuation\n");
     printf("——-\t——-\t—\t-\t——-\t———-\n");
     printf("%9d\t%9d\t%6d\t%5d\t%7d\t%11d\n",
          UpperLetters, LowerLetters, Digits, Space, Control,
          Punctuation);
     RealCount = (float) Count;
     printf ("%9.2f\t%9.2f\t%6.2f\t%5.2f\t%7.2f\t%11.2f\n",
          UpperLetters/RealCount, LowerLetters/RealCount,
     Digits/RealCount, Space/RealCount, Control/RealCount,
                                        Punctuation/RealCount);
     printf ("\n\nAnalysis program terminates here \n\n");
     return (0);
}
```

This program makes use of the inbuilt functions for checking characters which are available from the include file <ctype.h>. Notice the use of the control of the fields which are to be printed through the printf statements, e.g. %9d meaning print the integer for this specifier in a field nine columns. wide

2.6
C includes the pre- and post-increment/decrement operators as an aid to efficiency.

With regard to the two `for` loop code fragments you should have noticed that the first loop, which used the pre-increment operator on the loop control variable `Count`, ran from 1 to 10, whereas as the second ran from 0 to 10. The only difference was that pre-increment was used in the first loop and post-increment in the second. The pre-increment operator increments the value of `Count` before it is used; as `Count` is initialized to 0 when it is printed the first time through the loop, in the first loop the pre increment operator increments its value by 1 and then its value is printed. With the post-increment operator the current value of `Count` is printed first and then it is incremented.

Chapter 3

3.1

A somewhat trickier problem than it looks! Walk through the code and after each `if` statement write down what conditions held for you to have reached that point.

```c
#include <stdio.h>
#include <stdlib.h>

        /* The following shows parameters which
        will be used to pass copies of variables
        into the function */
void printorder(int anint, float afloat, char achar)
{
    if( anint <= afloat )
    {
        if( anint <= achar )
        {
            if( afloat <= achar )
            {
                printf("%d %.1f %c\n", anint, afloat, achar);
            }
            else
            {
                printf("%d %c %.1f\n", anint, achar, afloat);
            }
        }
        else
        {
            printf("%c %d %f\n", achar, anint, afloat);
        }
    }
```

```
        else if( afloat <= anint)
        {
             if( afloat <= achar )
             {
                 if( anint <= achar)
                 {
                         printf("%f %d %c\n", afloat, anint, achar);
                 }
                 else
                 {
                         printf("%f %c %d\n", afloat, achar, anint);
                 }
             }
             else
             {
                 printf("%c %f %d", achar, afloat, anint);
             }
        }
}


main()
{
      int anint;
      float afloat;
      char achar;

      /* This program prompts the user for
      values for the int float and char and calls the
      printorder() function*/

      printf("Input int float char, separated by a ");
      printf("single space only: ");
      scanf("%d%f %c", &anint, &afloat, &achar);
      printf("\n\n");
      printorder(anint, afloat, achar);
      exit(0);
}
```

3.2

The following shows an example implementation of the solution to this problem. Remember that there are many ways to solve the same problem so your solution may differ in detail:

```
/*******************************************************/
/* Simple program which presents a menu, users pick    */
```

```
/* options from menu, enter quantity of selected       */
/* items, and program calculates charge for individual*/
/* and total selections.  Uses a function to calculate*/
/* the amount for an individual item.                  */
/*****************************************************/

#include <stdio.h>

main()
{

            /* Function Prototypes */
        float GetPrice(int Item);
        float ItemCharge(float Price, int Quantity);
        void DisplayMenu(void);
        int GetItem(void);
        int GetQuantity(void);

            /* local variables     */
        int Item = '\0';
        int NumofItems = 0;
        float TotalCharge = 0.0;

            /* start of main program */

        DisplayMenu();
        while ((Item = GetItem()) != 'q')
        {

            TotalCharge += ItemCharge( GetPrice(Item),
                            (NumofItems += GetQuantity()));
            DisplayMenu();

        }

        printf("\n\nThe Total Charge for the %d Items \
        is %8.2f\n\n",NumofItems, TotalCharge);
        return(0);
} /* end main() */

int GetItem()
{
        /*********************************************/
        /* Function reads in a character validates it, */
        /* complains and reprompts if invalid, or      */
```

```
        /* returns a valid character to the caller.    */
        /***********************************************/

        int Reply;

        printf("\nPlease choose your drink [w,g,c,b,q]...>");
        do
        {
                switch(Reply = getchar())
                {
                        case 'w':
                        case 'g':
                        case C:
                        case 'b':
                        case 'q': {
                                return( Reply );
                                break;
                                }
                        default : {
                                printf("\n %c is an invalid input",
                                                        Reply);
                                printf("\n\nPlease choose your");
                                printf("drink [w,g,c,b,q]...> ");
                                break;
                                }
                }
        while (getchar() != '\n');
        } while (1);/* infinite loop ended by return in switch */
}

int GetQuantity(void)
{
        int Quantity;
        do
        {

                printf("\n\nHow many drinks do you require ..> ");
                scanf("%d", &Quantity);
                while (getchar() != '\n'); /* skip newline */
                if (Quantity < 0)
                {
                        printf("%d is invalid, positive whole");
                        printf("numbers only please\n");
                }
        } while (Quantity < 0);
```

```c
                return(Quantity);
}

float ItemCharge(float Price, int Quantity)
{
        return(Price * Quantity);
}

float GetPrice(int Item)
{
        float Price;

        switch(Item)
        {
                        /* Better to use constants for
                        the prices */
                case 'w' : {
                        Price = 12.20;
                        break;
                        }
                case 'g' : {
                        Price = 8.5;
                        break;
                        }
                case C : {
                        Price = 0.72;
                        break;
                        }
                case 'b' : {
                        Price = 12.12;
                        break;
                        }
        }
        return(Price);
}

void DisplayMenu(void)
{
        printf("\n\n\t\t\tDrinks Menu:\n\n");
        printf("\t\t\tWhiskey (w)\n\n");
        printf("\t\t\tGin   (g)\n\n");
        printf("\t\t\tCoke  (c)\n\n");
        printf("\t\t\tBrandy  (b)\n\n");
        printf("\t\t\tQuit  (q)\n\n");
}
```

3.3

The following show the functions implemented in a file called
charfuncs.c. A main() program is included just to test the functions:

```
#include <stdio.h>
#include <string.h>
#include <ctype.h>

int upper( char inchar )
{
        if(( inchar >= 'A') && ( inchar <='Z' ))
                return(1);
        else
                return(0);
}

int vowel( char inchar )
{
        char testchar;

        testchar = tolower( inchar );
        switch( testchar )
        {
        case 'a' :
        case 'e' :
        case 'i' :
        case 'o' :
        case 'u' : return(1);
        default  : return(0);
        }
}

char consonant( char inchar )
{
        if( isalpha( inchar ) && !vowel( inchar ))
                return(1);
        else
                return(0);
}

/* The following can be used to test the above functions */
main()
{
        int inchar;

        printf("input character> ");
```

```
            inchar = getchar();
            printf("\n\nupper = %d, vowel = %d, consonant = %d\n",
                        ((char)inchar), vowel((char)inchar),
                                    consonant((char)inchar));
}
```

You were asked to provide these functions for use by another programmer. You would achieve this by supplying a header file called charfuncs.h which contains the following function prototypes:

```
int upper(char);
int vowel(char);
int consonant(char);
```

If you now compile using:

```
cc -o charfuncs charfuncs.c
```

(with the main() program removed from charfuncs.c), then you can supply the charfuncs.o and charfuncs.h files to other programmers so that they can use the functions. They simply have to insert the line:

```
#include "charfuncs.h"
```

into their program and then include the charfuncs.o file on their compile line, e.g.

```
cc -o myprog myprog.c charfuncs.o
```

Other programmers cannot alter the implementations of the functions as there is no provided source (.c) file; this is kept by the programmer who created and is to maintain this library of functions.

Chapter 4

4.1
The following program shows how this can be achieved using a straightforward array of ten integers and appropriate for loops to control the array subscript value:

```
#include <stdio.h>

#define MAX 10

main()
```

```
{
        int array[MAX], index;

                /* input ten integers */
        printf("Enter 10 integers:\n");
                /* Notice that loop says (index < MAX)
                not (index <= MAX) */
        for(index = 0; index < MAX; index++)
        {
                printf("\nEnter integer number %d: ", index + 1);
                scanf("%d", &array[index]);
        }

                /* output array in reverse */
        printf("Array in revers is: ");
                /* Notice how index must start at MAX - 1 */
        for(index = MAX - 1; index >= 0; index--)
        {
                printf("%d ",array[index]);
        }
}
```

Here we use a fixed size array to hold the values read in from the keyboard. Notice that we place these values directly into the array by applying the address operator to the individual elements of this array, i.e. `&array[index];`. Also note that, when we prompt for each element to be entered, we also print the index of the element we are currently dealing with. This will give the person typing the data in an indication of how far through the input process they are. Once the the values are stored in an array, then we can print out the contents by accessing them in reverse order using a `for` which decrements the loop control variable.

4.2

The following shows how the input array of integers can be sorted either ascending by value or descending by value. The sort method employed here is the straightforward bubble sort. You may well have chosen one of the many other sort methods such as binary chop or shell short, which is fine. What is important is that the program works and correctly manipulates the arrays using subscripts.

```
#include <stdio.h>

#define MAX 10

main()
{
```

```c
int array[MAX], index, pass, temp, swap;
int direction = 0;

                        /* Enter 10 integers*/
printf("Enter 10 integers:\n");
for(index = 0; index < MAX; index++)
{
       printf("\nEnter an integer: ");
       scanf("%d", &array[index]);
}
                        /* Enter direction */
printf("\nEnter the sort direction as\n");
printf("ascending (1) or descending (2): ");
scanf("%d", &direction);

                        /* Set up passes for bubble sort */
for( pass = MAX; pass > 1; pass—)
{
swap = 0;
                        /* Set up pass through array */
for(index = 1; index < pass; index++)
{
                        /* sort for ascending */
       if( direction == 1)
       {
                        /* Check adjacent array elements */
             if(array[index] < array[index - 1])
             {
                   /* Swap */
                   temp = array[index];
                   array[index] = array[index - 1];
                   array[index - 1] = temp;
                   swap = 1;
             }
       }
                        /* sort for descending */
       else if( direction == 2)
       {
                        /* Check adjacent array elements */
             if(array[index] > array[index - 1])
             {
                   /* Swap */
                   temp = array[index];
                   array[index] = array[index - 1];
                   array[index - 1] = temp;
```

```
                              swap = 1;
                    }
            }
    }
                    /* if no swap occured - aleady sorted so
                              no more passes required */
    if( swap == 0)
            break;
    }
    printf("\n\nArray now is: ");
    for(index = 0; index < MAX; index++)
    {
            printf("%d ",array[index]);
    }
    printf("\n");
    return(0);
}
```

4.3

The following shows how the previous program was reimplemented using pointers rather than array subscripts:

```
#include <stdio.h>

#define MAX 10

main()
{
        int array[MAX], index, pass, temp, swap;
        int direction = 0;
        int *intptr;

                        /* Enter 10 integers*/
        printf("Enter 10 integers:\n");
        for(intptr = array, index = 1; index <= MAX; index++)
        {
                printf("\nEnter an integer: ");
                scanf("%d", intptr++);
        }

                        /* Enter direction */
        printf("\nEnter the sort direction as\n");
        printf("ascending (1) or descending (2): ");
        scanf("%d", &direction);

                        /* Set up passes for bubble sort */
```

```
for( pass = MAX; pass > 1; pass—)
{
        swap = 0;
                        /* Set up one pass */
        for(index = 1,intptr = array + 1; index < pass;
                intptr++,index++)
        {
                        /* sort for ascending */
                if( direction == 1)
                {
                        /* Check adjacent array elements */
                        if(*intptr < *(intptr - 1))
                        {
                        /* swap, notice use of pointers */
                                temp = *intptr;
                                *intptr = *(intptr - 1);
                                *(intptr - 1) = temp;
                                swap = 1;
                        }
                }
                        /* sort for descending */
                else if( direction == 2)
                {
                        /* Check adjacent array elements */
                        if(*intptr > *(intptr - 1))
                        {
                        /* swap */
                                temp = *intptr;
                                *intptr = *(intptr - 1);
                                *(intptr - 1) = temp;
                                swap = 1;
                        }
                }
        }
                        /* if no swap occured - aleady sorted so
                        no more passes required */
        if( swap == 0)
                break;
        }
                        /* Print out sorted array */
printf("\n\nArray now is: ");
for(intptr = array,index = 0; index < MAX; index++)
{
        printf("%d ",*intptr++);
}
```

```
            printf("\n");
            return(0);
    }
```

4.4

The following shows how this can be implemented – it is similar to the way that the string library function strcmp() is implemented. Again a main program is included to call and demonstrate these functions.

```
#include <stdio.h>


            /* pass pointers to strings - use const
            parameters as strings won't be altered */

int wordsame( const char *word1, const char *word2)
{
            /* Move through words while chars are same */
    for(; *word1 == *word2; ++word1, ++word2)
    {
            /* If we have reached null (in both strings) */
        if( *word1 == '\0')
            return(1);
    }
            /* Return zero as words weren't same */
    return(0);
}


main()
{
    char word1[10], word2[10];


            /* Enter words and discard preceeding and trailing
            blanks using scanf() */
    printf("Input word 1 :");
    scanf("%s", word1);
    printf("\n\nInput word 2 :");
    scanf("%s", word2);
            /* Output whether words were same */
    printf("\n\nWords are %s\n",
                    wordsame(word1,word2) ? "same" : "not same");
    return(0);
}
```

4.5

In terms of precedence ++, – and * have higher precedence than * and /, which in turn have higher precedence than + and –. With regard to associativity +, –, *(i.e. multiply), / have left to right associativity, whereas ++ ,– and * (i.e. dereference) have right to left associativity. To illustrate this consider the following expression :

```
*++IntPtr + Value- / Divisor;
```

Here the precedence laws say evaluation would occur as follows:

(I)   `(*++IntPtr)`
(ii) `(Value- / Divisor)`
(iii) (i) + (ii)

The associativity laws indicate that the expression

```
*++IntPtr
```

would be implemented as increment the pointer first and then get the contents of the memory location it now points to.

4.6

The following shows how these functions can be implemented using pointers. Included is a main program which demonstrates use of these functions.

```c
#include <stdio.h>

                    /* Notice the use of const parameters
                       as they are not changed in the function */
int inrange(const int input, const int min, const int max)
{
                    /* simple check if in range */
            return( input >= min && input <= max ? 1 : 0);

}

int charinset( char *string, const char inchar )
{
            int i;

                    /* Move through string to null */
            for(i = 0; *string != '\0'; string++, i++)
            {
                    /* If character found, return index */
                    if( *string == inchar )
                            return(i);
            }
                    /* Character not found */
```

```
                        return(-1);
}


int stringlength( const char *string )
{
        const char *charptr;

                        /* set pointer to start of array
                           and move through until null encountered */
        for(charptr = string; *charptr != '\0'; charptr++)
                ;

                /* Now return difference between pointer and
                address of start of string array */
                return(charptr - string);
}


main()
{
        printf("%d %d %d %d %d\n", inrange(4,1,6),
                                   inrange(7,1,6),
                                   charinset("hello",'l'),
                                   charinset("hello",'a'),
                                   stringlength("abcd"));
        return(0);
}
```

4.7

Pointer arithmetic allows manipulation to be made in terms of units of memory required for the type of data which a pointer points at. Thus, if an int is allocated to four bytes, a float eight bytes and a char one byte then adding one to an int pointer will increment the address it points to by four bytes, adding one to a float pointer will result in an increase of eight memory locations and adding one to a char pointer results in an increase of one memory location.

Chapter 5

5.1

```
#define MonthSize 10

struct Date
{
        int Day;
```

```
        char Month[MonthSize];
        int Year;
}
```

5.2

```
#define Size1 25

struct PersonnelRecord
{
        char Name[Size1];
        struct Date DateOfBirth;
        float Salary;
        int NHSnumber;
        char Position[Size1];
        struct Date DateOfJoining;
}
```

5.3

(I) Arrays allow you to group together objects of the same type, whereas structs allow you to group together logically related data which can be of different types. You can decalre arrays of structs and structs can themselves have fields which are arrays. A typical example of appropriate array usage would be a table of integers and for a struct the set of information relating to staff in a company, e.g. name, age, salary etc.

(ii) One struct for this information would be:

```
#define NameLen 25
#define PositionLen 12
#define MobilityLen 15
#define AddressLen 50
#define MaxStaff 50;
#define MaxPupils 50;
#define MaxFireExits 40

struct FireRegs
{
        int FloorNum;
        int RoomNum;    ˙
};

struct StaffRec
{
        char Name[NameLen];
        char Grade[PositionLen];
        float salary;
```

```
};

struct StaffData
{
        int NumOfStaff;
        struct StaffRec Staff[MaxStaff];
};

struct PupilRec
{
        char Name[NameLen];
        int Age;
        int ClassNum;
        int DeskNumber;
        char Mobility[MobilityLen];
};

struct PupilData
{
        int NumOfPupils;
        struct PupilRec Pupils[MaxPupils];
};

struct SchoolData
{
        char Category[PositionLen];
        char Name[NameLen];
        char Address[AddressLen];
        int RefNum;
        struct FireRegs FireExits[MaxFireExits];
        struct StaffData StaffData;
        struct PupilData ChildrenData;
};

struct SchoolData Schools[59];
```

Notice the use of constants to control the sizes of the character arrays which are scattered throughout the various struct definitions. It would of course be possible for string pointers to be used instead of arrays of char but these, though offering particular advantages, are often the cause of errors for novice C programmers. The solution offered above creates separate structs for the various components in the problem and then allows one struct to create a field which has a type that is itself another struct, thus embedding one struct within another.

(iii)
```
#include <string.h>

main ()
{
  int NumChairBoundPupils(struct SchoolData);

  return (0);
}


int NumChairBoundPupils(struct SchoolData ThisSchool)
{
        int Count = 0;
        int PupilTotal;
        struct PupilRec *PupilRecPtr = ThisSchool.ChildrenData.Pupils;

        while (PupilRecPtr)
        {
                if (strcmp(PupilRecPtr->Mobility, "WheelChairBound"))
                {
                        Count++;
                }
                PupilRecPtr++;
        }
        return(Count);
}
```

Notice the levels of indirection involved here when we pass an instance of the struct SchoolData to this function. We need to access the array of details for the school children and this is available by following the ChildrenData field to the Pupils array held under the field ChildrenData.Pupils. The processing after this is a simple sequential step through the Pupils array checking to see if the Mobility field has the value "WheelChairBound". The field ChildrenData.NumOfPupils holds the number of pupils in this class.

5.4
```
#include <stdio.h>
#include <string.h>

#define Size 10
#define NameLen 25
#define TitleLen 20
#define AddressLen 40
#define MaxEnumSize 11
```

```c
enum ArtisticCategory
{
        painting, sculpture, ceramic, craftwork, unknown
};

struct ExhibitRec
{
        char Title[TitleLen];
        char ArtistName[NameLen];
        char Address[AddressLen];
        enum ArtisticCategory Exhibit;
        float Price;
};

main()
{
        void GetExhibitData(struct ExhibitRec *);
        void PrintExhibitData(struct ExhibitRec *);

        struct ExhibitRec Exhibits[Size];
        struct ExhibitRec *ExhibitPtr;

        for (ExhibitPtr = Exhibits; ExhibitPtr <= &Exhibits[Size -
                                        1]; ExhibitPtr++)
        {
                GetExhibitData(ExhibitPtr);
        }
        for (ExhibitPtr = Exhibits; ExhibitPtr <= &Exhibits[Size -
                                        1]; ExhibitPtr++)
        {
                PrintExhibitData(ExhibitPtr);
        }
        return(0);
}

enum ArtisticCategory GetArtisticCategory(void)
{
        int Choice;
        enum ArtisticCategory ThisExhibit;

        printf("\n\nWhat is the Artistice Category of the exhibit :-
                                        \n\n");
        printf("\t1 - Painting\n\t2 - Sculpture\n\t3 - Ceramic\n\t4
                                        - Craft Work\n\n");
        printf("Select a Category ..> ");
```

```
        scanf("%d", &Choice);
        switch (Choice)
        {
                case 1: {ThisExhibit = painting;
                        break;
                                }
                case 2: {ThisExhibit = sculpture;
                        break;
                                }
                case 3: {ThisExhibit = ceramic;
                        break;
                                }
                case 4: {ThisExhibit = craftwork;
                        break;
                                }
                default: { ThisExhibit = unknown;
                        break;
                                }
        }
        return(ThisExhibit);
}


void GetExhibitData(struct ExhibitRec *ExhibitPtr)
{
        enum ArtisticCategory GetArtisticCategory(void);
        char ReturnKey;

        printf("\n\nEnter the Title of the exhibit ..>");
        gets(ExhibitPtr->Title);
        printf("\nEnter the Artist's Name ..> ");
        gets(ExhibitPtr->ArtistName);
        printf("\nEnter the Artist's address ..>");
        gets(ExhibitPtr->Address);
        ExhibitPtr->Exhibit = GetArtisticCategory();
        printf("\nEnter the price of the exhibit ..>");
        scanf("%f", &ExhibitPtr->Price);
        ReturnKey = getchar();
}


void ConvertEnum(enum ArtisticCategory Object, char *Category)
{

        switch (Object)
        {
                case painting : {strcpy(Category,"Painting");
```

```
                                        break;
                                }
                case sculpture : {strcpy(Category,"Sculpture");
                                        break;
                                }
                case ceramic : {strcpy(Category,"Ceramic");
                                        break;
                                }
                case craftwork : {strcpy(Category,"Craft Work");
                                        break;
                                }
                default : {strcpy(Category,"Unknown");
                                        break;
                                }
        }

}


void PrintExhibitData(struct ExhibitRec *Exhibits)
{
        void ConvertEnum(enum ArtisticCategory, char *);
        char Category[MaxEnumSize];

        printf("\n\nExhibit details are as follows:-\n\n");
        printf("Title\t\t%s\n", Exhibits->Title);
        ConvertEnum(Exhibits->Exhibit,Category);
        printf("Category\t%s\n", Category);
        printf("Price\t\t%8.2f\n", Exhibits->Price);
        printf("Artist's Name\t%s\n", Exhibits->ArtistName);
        printf("Artist's Address\t%s\n\n", Exhibits->Address);
        printf("End of details for this exhibit\n\n");
}
```

This problem is concerned once again with the need to create and use data structures, but it also forces us to examine the practicalities involved in using enumerated types In particular, we see the need to provide functions both to get values for variables of `enum` types and to transform them into the enumeration value. Similarly, when the value of an enumerated variable is displayed, there is a need to transform into a usable value. These actions are carried out the functions `GetArtisticCategory()` and `ConvertEnum()`

5.5

```
/* Creation of a struct and then using that struct in a program    */

#include <stdio.h>
```

```
#include <string.h>
#define Size 15
#define Maxcars 1

struct CarDetails
{
        char Manufacturer[Size];
        char Model [Size];
        int Price;
        int Age;
        int Milage;
        char Colour[Size];
        int EngineSize;
};


/******************************************************************/

main()
{
        struct CarDetails GetCarDetails(void);
        void BuyerRequirements(char *, int *);
        void SearchForCar(struct CarDetails *, char *, int );

        struct CarDetails CarBase[Maxcars];
        int Count, Limit;

        char Maker[Size];
        printf("\n\nInitialising the CarDetails Database:\n\n");
        for (Count = 0; Count < Maxcars; Count++)
        {
                CarBase[Count] = GetCarDetails();
        }
        BuyerRequirements(Maker, &Limit);
        SearchForCar(CarBase, Maker, Limit);
        printf("\n\n\tProgram terminates here\n\n");
        return(0);
}

struct CarDetails GetCarDetails(void)
{
        struct CarDetails TempCar;

        printf("\n\nPlease enter the following data :-\n\n");
        printf("\n\tManufacturer\t...>");
        scanf("%s", TempCar.Manufacturer);
```

```
        printf("\n\t Model\t\t...>");
        scanf("%s", TempCar.Model);
        printf("\n\tPrice\t\t...>");
        scanf("%d", &TempCar.Price);
        printf("\n\t Age\t\t...>");
        scanf("%d", &TempCar.Age);
        printf("\n\t Milage\t\t...>");
        scanf("%d", &TempCar.Milage);
        printf("\n\t Body Colour\t...>");
        scanf("%s", TempCar.Colour);
        printf("\n\t  Engine Size\t\t...>");
        scanf("%d", &TempCar.EngineSize);
        return(TempCar);
}


void BuyerRequirements(char *Maker, int *Limit)
{
        printf("\n\nPlease specify the following details:-\n\n");
        printf("\tWhich Manufacturer do you prefer ...> ");
        scanf("%s", Maker);
        printf("\n\n\tWhat is your upper limit for price ...> ");
        scanf("%d", Limit);
}


void SearchForCar(struct CarDetails *CarBase, char *Maker, int Limit)
{
        void DisplayCarDetails(struct CarDetails *);
        struct CarDetails *CarPtr = CarBase;

        printf("\n\nSuitable Cars are:-\n\n");
        printf(" Manufacturer        Model   Price Age   Milage
                                Colour    Engine\n");
        printf("  _____        _____ _____ __   ____
                                _____  _____\n");
        for (; CarPtr <= &CarBase[Maxcars - 1]; CarPtr++)
        {
                if ( (strcmp(CarPtr->Manufacturer, Maker) == 0) &&
                                (CarPtr->Price <= Limit))
                {
                        DisplayCarDetails(CarPtr);
                }
        }
}


void DisplayCarDetails(struct CarDetails * CarPtr)
```

```
{
        printf("\n%15s %15s %6d %2d %10d %15s %5d\n",
                CarPtr->Manufacturer,   CarPtr->Model,  CarPtr->Price,
                CarPtr->Age,            CarPtr->Milage, CarPtr->Colour,
                CarPtr->EngineSize);
}
```

In this example you are asked to create and manipulate a simple database using structs as the basis of the record descriptions.

5.6

```
#include <stdio.h>
#include <string.h>

#define Size1 25
#define Size2 50
#define MaxLoan 10
#define NumBorrowers 5
#define NumBooks 5
#define LoanPeriod 28
#define FineRate 10.0

enum BookType { ref, classical, nonfiction, thriller, adventure,
                                                    sci_fi};

struct Book
{
        char Title [Size1];
        char Author [Size1];
        int BookNum;
        int OnLoan;
        enum BookType Category;
        int DueDate;
} ;

struct BorrowerDetails
{
        char Name[Size1];
        char Address[Size2];
        int NumBooksonLoan;
        struct Book *BooksOnLoan[MaxLoan];
        float FinesOwed;
} ;

main()
```

```
{
      void IssueBook(struct BorrowerDetails *, struct Book*);
      void ReturnBook(struct BorrowerDetails *, struct Book *);
      void DisplayBookDetails(struct Book *);
      void DisplayBorrowerDetails(struct BorrowerDetails *);
      static struct BorrowerDetails Borrowers[NumBorrowers] =
            {   {"Peter    Smith",    "21   Lilac   Avenue   Redcar",
0,{NULL,NULL,NULL,NULL,NULL,NULL,NULL,NULL,NULL,NULL}, 0.0},
            {"John White", "14, Linden Avenue HartBurn",0,{NULL} ,0.0},
            {"Paul Brown", "27, Snow Park, Haydock", 0,{NULL} ,0.0}
            };

      static struct Book Books[NumBooks] =
            { {"Persuasion", "Jane Austen", 1234, 0, classical,0},
            {"Hard Times","Charles Dickens", 1379, 0, classical, 0},
            {"The Moonstone", "Wilkie Collins",1694, 0, classical, 0}
            };

      struct BorrowerDetails *BorrowerPtr = Borrowers;
      struct Book *BookPtr = Books;

      printf("\nIssue Book 1\n");
      IssueBook(BorrowerPtr, BookPtr++);
      DisplayBorrowerDetails(BorrowerPtr);
      printf("\nIssue Book 2\n");
      IssueBook(BorrowerPtr, BookPtr);
      DisplayBorrowerDetails(BorrowerPtr);
      printf("\nReturn Book 1\n");
      ReturnBook(BorrowerPtr, —BookPtr);
      DisplayBorrowerDetails(BorrowerPtr);
      return(0);
}

void IssueBook(struct BorrowerDetails *BorrowerPtr, struct Book
                                                    *BookPtr)
{
      int Today();

      if (BorrowerPtr->NumBooksonLoan < MaxLoan)
      {
            BorrowerPtr->BooksOnLoan[BorrowerPtr-
                  >NumBooksonLoan] = BookPtr;
            BorrowerPtr->NumBooksonLoan++;
            BookPtr->OnLoan = 1;
            BookPtr->DueDate = Today() + LoanPeriod;
```

```
        }
        else
        {
                printf("\n\n%s has the maximum number of books on
                                                loan \n");
                printf("and cannot borrow any more.\n\n");
        }
}


void ReturnBook(struct BorrowerDetails *BorrowerPtr, struct Book
                                                *BookPtr)
{
        float CalculateFines(struct Book *);

        struct Book **TempPtr = BorrowerPtr->BooksOnLoan;
        int Count = 0;

        while ((Count <= BorrowerPtr->NumBooksonLoan) && (*TempPtr
                                                != BookPtr))
        {
                *TempPtr++;
        }
        if (*TempPtr = BookPtr)
        {
                BookPtr->OnLoan = 0;
                BorrowerPtr->FinesOwed = CalculateFines(BookPtr);
                while (Count != BorrowerPtr->NumBooksonLoan)
                {
                        BorrowerPtr->BooksOnLoan[Count] =
                                BorrowerPtr->BooksOnLoan[Count + 1];
                        Count++;
                }
                BorrowerPtr->NumBooksonLoan--;
        }
        else
        {
                printf("\n\n%s is not listed as being on loan to
                                                %s\n\n",
                        BookPtr->Title, BorrowerPtr->Name);
        }
}


int Today(void)
{
        static TimeInDays = 1096;
```

```
            return(TimeInDays++);
}


float CalculateFines(struct Book *BookPtr)
{
        float Fines;
        int WeeksOverDue = 0, OverDue = 0;

        OverDue = BookPtr->DueDate - Today();
        if (OverDue < 0)
        {
                WeeksOverDue = OverDue / 7;
                if (OverDue % 7)
                {
                        WeeksOverDue++;
                }
        }
        Fines = (float) WeeksOverDue * FineRate;
        return(Fines);
}


void DisplayBookDetails(struct Book *BookPtr)
{
        printf("%12s %15s %6d %6d\n", BookPtr->Title, BookPtr-
                                                        >Author,
                BookPtr->BookNum, BookPtr->OnLoan);
}


void DisplayBorrowerDetails(struct BorrowerDetails *Borrower)
{
        int Count, ReturnKey;

        printf("\n\n      Name            Address          Num Loaned
                                            Fines Owed\n");
        printf("      ____          _____        _____
                                      _____\n\n");
        printf("%12s %12s %6d %12.2f\n",Borrower->Name, Borrower-
                                                        >Address,
                Borrower->NumBooksonLoan,Borrower->FinesOwed);
        printf("\n\nBooks on loan to this borrower:-\n\n");
        printf("\n\n    Title          Author      ISBN  On Loan");
        printf("\n      _____          _____      ___  __
                                      ____\n\n");

        for (Count = 0; Count < Borrower->NumBooksonLoan; Count++)
```

```
        {
                DisplayBookDetails(Borrower->BooksOnLoan[Count]);
        }
        ReturnKey = getchar();
}
```

This example involves the use of structures, the making and breaking of links from one structure to another, e.g. from a borrower to a book and the associated referencing. The very simplistic function Today() is added for completeness; a better approach would be to use the date facility available from the operating system of the machine that you are using, e.g. DOS, UNIX. In this solution the arrays for the Borrowers and Books are initialized within the program and as such 'static arrays' are used to hold the relevant information.

Chapter 6

6.1

```
#include <stdio.h>
#include <stdlib.h>

struct UniqueData
{
        int Occurs;
        int Number;
        struct UniqueData *Next;
};

main()
{
        int *GetArrayDetails(int);
        struct UniqueData *AnalyseArray(int*, int);
        void PrintListDetails(struct UniqueData*);
        void PrintArrayDetails(int*, int);

        struct UniqueData *List;
        int *Array;
        int ArraySize;

        printf("\n\nHow many elements are needed for the array ..> ");
        scanf("%d", &ArraySize);
        Array = GetArrayDetails(ArraySize);
        List = AnalyseArray(Array, ArraySize);
        PrintListDetails(List);
```

```
            return(0);
}


int * GetArrayDetails(int ArraySize)
{
        int   Count;
        int *ArrayHead, *ArrayPtr;

        ArrayHead = (int *) calloc(ArraySize, sizeof(int));
        for (Count = 0, ArrayPtr = ArrayHead; Count < ArraySize;
            Count++, ArrayPtr++)
        {
                printf("\n\tEnter value for element %2d ..>", Count
                                                            + 1);
                scanf("%d", ArrayPtr);
        }
        return(ArrayHead);
}


struct UniqueData *AnalyseArray(int *Array, int ArraySize)
{
        int Count;
        struct UniqueData *ListHead, *PreviousPtr, *ListPtr,
                                                    *TempPtr;
        int ReturnKey;

        ListHead = NULL;
        for (Count = 0, ListPtr = ListHead; Count < ArraySize;
                                                    Count++)
        {
                printf("\nDealing with %d\n", Array[Count]);
                if (ListHead == NULL)
                {
                        printf("\nFirst element %d\n", Array[Count]);
                        ListHead = malloc(sizeof(struct UniqueData));
                        ListHead->Number = Array[Count];
                        ListHead->Occurs = 1;
                        ListHead->Next = NULL;
                }
                else
                {
                        printf("\nSearching for a match:- %d",
                                                Array[Count]);
                        ListPtr = ListHead;
                        PreviousPtr = ListHead;
```

```
                        while ((ListPtr->Next != NULL) && (ListPtr-
                                    >Number != Array[Count] ))
                {
                        printf("\nMatching %d with %d",
                                ListPtr->Number,Array[Count]);
                        PreviousPtr = ListPtr;
                        ListPtr = ListPtr->Next;
                }
                if (ListPtr->Number == Array[Count])
                                        /*found a match */
                {
                        printf("\nFound a match so increment
                                                occurs\n");
                        ListPtr->Occurs++;
                }
                else if (!ListPtr->Next) /* no match found */
                {
                        printf("\nNo match on the list - add
                                                at end\n");
                        ListPtr->Next = malloc(sizeof(struct
                                                UniqueData));
                        ListPtr->Next->Number = Array[Count];
                        ListPtr->Next->Occurs = 1;
                        ListPtr->Next->Next = NULL;
                }
            }
            ReturnKey = getchar();
        }
        return(ListHead);
}


void PrintListDetails(struct UniqueData *List)
{
        printf("\n\nThe list details are :-\n\n");
        if (List == NULL)
        {
                printf("\n\nThere are no elements to be dealt
                                                with.\n\n");
        }
        else if (List->Next == NULL)
        {
                printf("%6d occurs %6d times\n",
                        List->Number, List->Occurs);
        }
        else
```

```
        {
                do
                {
                printf("%6d occurs %6d times\n",
                        List->Number, List->Occurs);
                List = List->Next;
                } while (List);
        }
        printf("\n\nEnd of list Details\n\n");
}
```

This problem requires you to read a set of values into an array, something that should be very familiar to you already and then to analyse the contents of that array and dynamically create a linked list to hold the results of that analysis. Note that a new element for the list is not created until we are quite certain that the value we are dealing with does not exist on the list.

Chapter 7

7.1
The following shows how this file copy program can be implemented to append one file onto another. Notice the way that error conditions have been trapped particularly when dealing with files, as problems can often occur, e.g. no space left, file doesn't exist, haven't got permissions to use file etc.

```
#include <stdio.h>
#include <errno.h>
#include <stdlib.h>

main(int argc, char *argv[])
{
        int achar;
        FILE *fptr1, *fptr2;

        if( argc != 3)
        {
                printf("Wrong number of arguments\n");
                exit(0);
        }
        if((fptr1 = fopen(argv[1], "a")) == NULL)
        {
                perror(argv[1]);
                exit(0);
        }
```

```
        if((fptr2 = fopen(argv[2], "r")) == NULL)
        {
                perror(argv[2]);
        exit(0);
        }
        while((achar = fgetc(fptr2)) != EOF)
        {
                fputc(achar,fptr1);
        }
        fclose(fptr1);
        fclose(fptr2);
        exit(0);
}
```

7.2
The following shows how a file can be manipulated *in situ* – no trivial task you'll probably agree!

```
#include <stdio.h>
#include <errno.h>
#include <string.h>
#include <stdlib.h>

#define MAXLINE 134

main()
{
        FILE *fptr;
        char name[MAXLINE],word[MAXLINE];
        char line[MAXLINE],*charptr = NULL;
        int count;
        long filepos = 0;

        printf("Input file name: ");
        scanf("%s", name);
        printf("\nInput word to be blanked: ");
        scanf("%s",word);
                            /* Open file for update, read and write
                            in binary mode*/
        if((fptr = fopen(name, "rb+")) == NULL)
        {
                perror(name);
                exit(0);
        }
                            /* While there are lines in file
```

```
                              get a line */
        while( fgets(line, MAXLINE - 1, fptr) != NULL)
        {
                        /* While we can find word in the line */
                while((charptr = strstr(line, word)) != NULL)
                {
                        /* Obtain current position from start of  file*/
                        filepos = ftell(fptr);
                        /* Reposition write position to start of
                        word found in file  using pointer
                        arithmetic and known line length*/
                        fseek(fptr, (long)filepos - ((strlen(line)
                                - (charptr - line))), SEEK_SET);
                        /* Blank out word with X's in
                        both file and line array */
                        for(count = 1; count <= strlen(word); count++)
                        {
                                *charptr++ = 'X';
                                fputc('X',fptr);
                        }
                        /* Move read position back to end
                        line just processed */
                        fseek(fptr, filepos, SEEK_SET);
                        /* Force file changes to be written
                        to disk from memory */
                        fflush(fptr);
                }
        }
        fclose(fptr);
        printf("\nProgram finished\n");
        exit(0);
}
```

Appendix A

Trigraphs

The essential point regarding trigraphs is that any unsupported character can be used by referring to the table of trigraphs given in the ANSI standard and using the appropriate three-character sequence. For example the # is a pretty important character in C programming and, if the machine character set does not provide it, then including header files will be difficult. The ANSI standard has a trigraph for this character and it is:

??=Thus each preprocessor directive would start with ??= instead of #. All Trigraphs are three-character sequences of which the first two are ??. These notes will make no further reference to trigraphs other than to refer you to either text books on C Programming or the ANSI Standard for the C Programming Language for further details.

Appendix B

Operator precedence and associativity

The following shows the order of precedence of C operators. Note that highest precedence is at the top of the table.

Operators	Associativity
( ) [ ] -> .	left to right
! ~ ++ -- + - * (type) & sizeof	right to left*
* / %	left to right
+ - (i.e. binary operators add and subtract)	left to right
<< >>	left to right
< <= > >=	left to right
== !=	left to right
&	left to right
^	left to right
|	left to right
&&	left to right
||	left to right
?:	right to left
= += -= *= /= %= &= ^= |= <<= >>=	right to left
,	left to right

* *Note*: These are all unary operators.

Remember that associativity is not always left to right.

Just to recap what we mean by left-to-right associativity: the following brackets show how operators of the same precedence are executed for a left-to-right associativity:

`((5 * 6) / 3)` becomes `(30 / 3)` becomes `10`

Appendix C

Type conversion, coercion and casting

Conversion is an implicit action applied by several operators such that their operands all assume the same type. Where a value is converted there is no change to that value or its representation. Here is a table of the normal arithmetic conversions:

> IF either operand has type `long double` then the other operand is converted to `long double`
>
> ELSE if either operand has type `double` then the other operand is converted to `double`
>
> ELSE if either operand has type `float` then the other operand is converted to `float`
>
> ELSE if either operand has type `unsigned long int` then the other is converted to `unsigned long int`
>
> ELSE if either operand has type `long int` and the other operand has type `unsigned int` then
> if a `long int` can represent all the values of an `unsigned int` then the `unsigned int` is converted to `long int`
> Otherwise both operands are converted to type `unsigned long int`
>
> ELSE if either operand has type `long int` then the other is converted to `long int`
>
> ELSE if either operand has type `unsigned int` then the other is converted to `unsigned int`
>
> ELSE both operands have type `int`.

The priority of conversions is from the top of this table down to the bottom.

Coercion is the result of explicitly applying the cast operator to some value or the result of an expression. The effect is to produce a value of the specifed type, although the original value and its representation remain unchanged.

Appendix D

The C preprocessor

This facility was originally added to earlier versions of C to cope with a number of omissions, e.g. constant definitions. The ANSI standard has both provided a definition for the common preprocessor directives and also added several further directives which appeared to be well used within the more widely found variants.

Without the standard use of directives other than #include and #define, the # family created great portability problems due to their different implementations. The standard is not unduly concerned with backwards compatibility in the preprocessor area and should improve the portability of code written to conform with it.

Essentially the preprocessor works by scanning the source code for directives and then invoking the actions indicated by any directive it finds. Most programmers can use the #include, #define and #if family of directives with great effectiveness. The scope of a directive is effectively from the point in the source file where it is met to either the end of the file or until it is inactivated by an #undef or #endif etc. This is quite different to the block-based scope rules of C.

Any line which begins with a # is taken to be a directive. The convention is to place # in the first column of a directive line although this is not actually necessary. Each directive should be written on a single, separate line; you cannot have directives which span more than one line (again quite different from C code).

The directives

Directive	Meaning
#include	include a source file
#define	define a macro
#undef	undefine a macro
#if	conditionally compile what follows
#ifdef	conditionally compile what follows
#ifndef	conditionally compile what follows
#elif	conditionally compile what follows
#else	conditionally compile what follows
#endif	end of code in conditional compilation
#line	control current line number

```
#error              display error message
#Pragma             user defined implementations
#                   null directive
```

An explanation and associated examples of these directive follows.

The null directive

```
#
```

This is simply a line containing the # character and it has no effect. It can be used to introduce spacing within more complex directives.

The macro directive

```
#define
```

Macros are of two types, either a simple text substitution or a more complex function like substitution. For example:

```
#define STEAM   212
#define MAX (First, Second)     (First >= Second : First ? Second)
```

In each case once the #define directive is met all subsequent reference to "STEAM" are replaced by 212, and all function calls of the form MAX (a,b) are replaced (a > b = a ? b).

The simple form of macro substitution is C's mechanism for declaring constants. Again there is a convention that the text is written in upper case to indicate that it is a macro. It is also usual to place the directive at the head of a source file and so the macro is visible throughout the entire file. However macros can be defined anywhere within a source file and they will be usable from that point onwards within the file.

The function-like macro form is a way of achieving in-line expansion, but it is notoriously riddled with pitfalls for the unwary. In particular, the parameters which can be passed are a source of much heartache. Consider the following:

```
#define  SQUARE (X)   ((X) * (X))

      * IntPtr  =  10:
      Square((*IntPtr)++);
```

The substitution would produce

```
(((*IntPtr)++) * ((*IntPtr)++));
```

which it is hoped you can see would result in 10 * 11 and NOT 10 * 10 as might be required.

Don't use arguments which produce side effects like those in the example above. Do be careful when constructing and using function-like macros.

Undefining macros
#undef
The visibility of a macro is from the point in the source file where the `#define` is met to the end of file. If you wish to use the macro name for other purposes then you can undefine the macro allowing you to use the name as required.

Including header files
#include
Where the `#include` directive is met it is replaced with the contents of the indicated file, i.e. the file is inserted at that point in the file. Again it is usual to place `#include` directives at the head of a file but this does not have to be the case.

There are two forms of the `#include` specifically:

```
#include <standard header file>
#include "user defined headers"
```

The use of `<....>` tells the compiler to look in one of several predefined directories for the given file. For example

```
#include <stdio.h>
```

tells the compiler to look in the standard place (typically /usr/include on UNIX systems) for the header file `stdio.h`. Placing the file name in "...." tells the compiler to look in the same working directory, or it can be an absolute or relative path indicating where the file is to be found.

The conditional compilation directives.
#if #ifdef #ifndef #elif #else #endif
These allow programmers the extremely useful facility of controlling which parts of a program are compiled into the executable file. Why is this useful? Let us consider two examples:

Conditional compilation lets you build in debugging statements as you write the code so that during testing and development you can incorporate statements which generate trace information, print out variable values and so forth. Once the code is accepted, the debugging code can be excluded from the executable file, but it is left in the source code. Subsequent maintenance and testing is then much easier to perform.

A second example arises where code is intended to run on several different machines and where there is machine specific code needed for each machine. One solution would be to have separate source-code files for each machine, but this compounds the problem of keeping all such files to the same version. A better solution is to have one file which has the machine-specific code for all the machines and use conditional compilation to control what is included in the executable file.

For information concerning the other directives we refer you to the ANSI standard.

Appendix E

The standard ANSI (ISO) C libraries

The ANSI C standard includes a set of standard libraries which can be used in a consistent and portable manner across all ANSI conformant C compilers/linkers. You will already be familiar with many of the libraries and functions, having met them previously in context as you progressed through the chapters of this book. This appendix will serve to present a brief synopsis of those libraries not met elsewhere in the book but which may be required during your C software development. The treatment here will not be exhaustive but will present each library along with some example functions to illustrate the nature of the particular library. For a more detailed treatment you are referred to your manuals where a full description of the standard library functions is to be found.

Functions from the standard libraries are used by including the appropriate header file and it is therefore often found that a particular library is described by its header. This is done even though the headers only usually contain function prototypes, data structures, macros, types and constants necessary to link code from the corresponding binary code libraries. In keeping with this we will present a list of the header files and under these a description of the typical functions to be found.

The headers for the standard function libraries are as follows:

<assert.h>	<float.h>	<math.h>	<stdarg.h>	<stdlib.h>
<ctype.h>	<limits.h>	<setjmp.h>	<stddef.h>	<string.h>
<errno.h>	<locale.h>	<signal.h>	<stdio.h>	<time.h>

Input and output – <stdio.h>
These functions were covered in Chapter 7 and include formatted input/output, e.g. `fprintf()`, character-based input/output, e.g. `fgetc()`, file positioning, direct access, e.g. `ftell()` and file error functions, e.g. `feof()`.

Character class testing – <ctype.h>
The following functions return an `int` which is non-zero if condition is true and zero otherwise:

Function	Condition
`isalpha(c)`	upper or lower case alphabetic
`isalnum(c)`	upper or lower case alphabetic or decimal digit
`iscntrl(c)`	control character
`isdigit(c)`	decimal digit
`isgraph(c)`	printable character excepting space
`islower(c)`	lower case alphabetic
`isupper(c)`	upper case alphabetic
`isprint(c)`	printable character including space
`ispunct(c)`	printable character except alphabetic space or digit
`isspace(c)`	space linefeed formfeed tab carriage return or vertical tab
`isxdigit(c)`	hexadecimal digit

In each case `c` is an unsigned `char` converted to `int` or `EOF`.

String handling functions – `<string.h>`

The following are most useful in handling strings, but remember a string is a null-terminated array of characters – if the null is missing these functions will fail.

`char *strcpy(char *s1, const char *s2)`	copy string `s2` onto end of `s1` including `null`, return `s1`
`char *strncpy(char *s1, const char *s2, int n)`	copy at most *n* characters from `s2` onto `s1`, return `s1`
`char *strcat(char *s1, const char *s2)`	concatenate `s2` onto `s1`, return `s1`
`int strcmp(const char *s1, const char *s2)`	compare `s1` and `s2` return zero if same, non-zero first character difference otherwise
`char *strchr(const char s1, char c)`	return pointer to first occurence of `c` in `s1` and `null` otherwise
`char *strrchr(const char s1, char s)`	as `strchr()` but last occurence
`size_t strlen(const char s1)`	return length of `s1`

Other more specialized functions include `strspn()`, `strcspn()`, `strpbrk()`, `strstr()`, `strerror()` and `strtok()` – refer to your manuals for further details of these.

194   APPENDIX E – THE STANDARD ANSI (ISO) C LIBRARIES

There also exists a group of functions which will handle objects in memory, not just strings and these include `memcpy()`, `memmove()`, `memcmp()`, `memchr()` and `memset()` – again refer to your manuals for further information regarding these functions.

Mathematical functions – `<math.h>`

These provide all the usual mathematical functions:

- trigonometric functions – `sin()`, `cos()`, `tan()` etc.;
- log and power functions – `log()`, `log10()`, `pow()` etc.;
- squareroot – `sqr();`
- rounding functions – `floor()`, `ceil()` etc.

and several other functions. Again all these will be listed in your manuals and are straightforward to use on the whole.

Utility functions – `<stdlib.h>`

The functions provided here fall into groups:

- memory functions – `malloc()`, `calloc()` etc. which were met in Chapter 6;
- conversion functions – some of which include:

```
int atoi(const char *s1)        convert digits to int
double atof(const char *s1)     convert real-number digits to double
long atol(const char *s1)       convert digits to long
```

Again for some of the more obscure functions available refer to your manuals.

- calls to the operating environment, e.g.

```
void exit(int status)           terminate after flushing and closing file
                                streams returning status value to the
                                environment
int system(const char *s1)      pass the the string s1 to the environment
                                for execution
char *getenv(const char *s1)    return environment string for s1
                                environment variable
```

- miscellaneous:

  Functions for binary search (`bsearch()`) and sorting of arrays (`qsort()`).

  Functions to return absolute values of int (`abs()`) and long (`labs()`) arguments.

  Functions to derive the quotient and remainder of an int division (`div()`) or long division (`ldiv()`).

Date and time functions – `<time.h>`

Within `<time.h>` is declared a `struct tm` used by some of the time functions:

```
struct tm{
        int tm_sec;    /* seconds */
        int tm_min;    /* minutes */
        int tm_hour;   /* hours after midnight */
        int tm_mday;   /* day of month */
        int tm_mon;    /* month */
        int tm_year;   /* year since 1990 */
        int tm_wday;   /* days since Sunday – 0..6 */
        int tm_yday;   /* days since Jan 1st */
        int tm_isdst;  /* flag for daylight saving time */
        }
```

The following functions also use two types – `clock_t` and `time_t` to hold times. `time_t` holds the number of seconds since 00:00:00 on 1 January 1970.

`clock_t clock(void)`	return processor time for execution. Use `clock/CLOCKS_PER_SEC` to obtain time in seconds
`time_t time(time_t *tim)`	return number of seconds since 00:00:00 on 1 January 1970
`double difftime(time_t tim1, time_t tim2)`	difference in seconds between `tim2` and `tim1`
`time_t mktime(struct tm *tptr)`	convert time in structure to secs since 00:00:00 1 January 1970
`char *asctime(const struct tm *tptr)`	convert time in structure to form `Mon Jan  9 12:34:56 1994\n\0`
`char *ctime(const time_t *tim)`	convert `tim` to local time
`struct tm *gmtime(const time_t *tim)`	convert `tim` to greenwich mean time
`struct tm *localtime(const time_t *tim)`	convert `tim` to local time

To produce a customized format you can use `strftime()` which uses a `struct tm` to build a date/time formatted string – see your manuals for details.

Implementation dependent limits – `<limits.h>` and `<float.h>`

Refer to these header files to find limits such as maximum `int` or smallest `float` etc.

Generally less used standard functions groups
The following groups of functions are used in less common specific situations and you are referred to your manuals for further details of these function groups.

`<assert.h>`	diagnostics to add macros to programs
`<stdarg.h>`	functions to use variable argument lists along the lines of the `printf()` function call
`<setjmp.h>`	functions to allow non-local jumps in programs
`<signal.h>`	facilities to handle software interrupts such as termination requests or arithmetic exceptions

Index